FIVE - STAR

★ ★ ★ ★ ★

BASKETBALL

Edited by

ED SCHILLING • HOWARD GARFINKEL

MASTERS PRESS

A Division of Howard W. Sams & Co.

(A Division of Howard W. Sams & Co.)
2647 Waterfront Pkwy. E. Drive, Suite 100'
Indianapolis, IN 46214

10 9 8 7 6 5 4 3   97 98 99 00

Library of Congress Cataloging-in-Publication Data
Five-star basketball / edited by Ed Schilling and Howard Garfinkel.
   p. cm.
ISBN 0-940279-58-4
1. Basketball - Social Aspects - United States. 2. Basketball players - United States - Conduct of life. 3. Five-star (Pa. and Va.: Basketball camp) I. Schilling Ed, 1966-. II. Garfinkel, Howard.
GV889.26.F58   1993   93-13318
796.323'0973-dc20   CIP

Credits

Editor: Mark Montieth.

Cover design: Christy Pierce.

Front cover photographs provided by the publicity departments at Duke University, the University of Kentucky and the Detroit Pistons.

Inside photographs courtesy of North Carolina State University; Miami of Ohio; Xavier University; University of Kentucky; Indiana University; Philadelphia 76ers; Harvard University; CBS; Detroit Pistons; Indiana Pacers; ESPN; University of Southern California; Louisiana State University; New Jersey Nets; Duke University; Charlotte Hornets.

Acknowledgments

Completing this book required the help of many people. I would like to thank some of those who have been so helpful to me, not only with regard to this book but in all areas of my life.

First and foremost, I want to publicly thank God for all that He has done in my life and for the many blessings that He has graciously bestowed upon me.

Next, I'd like to thank my wife, Shawn, who has been a great help with various aspects of this book. Giving up the computer time during her final year in law school is much appreciated. Also, I'd like to thank my family, who taught me the sacrifice and dedication needed to take on a project such as this one.

Finally, I'd like to thank my second family — Five-Star Basketball Camp. Without Will Klein and Howard Garfinkel, this book would obviously not be possible. Also, thanks especially to Mr. Garfinkel, who has been at times my second father, at times my advisor, but most of all my friend.

Thanks again to all those mentioned and unmentioned who have contributed to Five-Star Basketball.

ED SCHILLING

Foreword

Five-Star Basketball is more than a compilation of outstanding lectures — it is a lifetime of insights, inspiring stories and advice from some of the world's most respected and recognized people in the world of basketball.

Each of the lectures included in this book was presented at the Five-Star Basketball Camp before hundreds of high school kids during the 1970's, '80's and '90's. Some of the speakers were in the beginning stages of their careers at the time the lectures in this book were presented (Jim Valvano with Iona and George Raveling with Washington State, for example), and while their teams have changed, the messages still hold true. Their ideas and philosophies have made them successful in basketball, and hopefully will contribute to the success and enjoyment of the reader.

Regretfully, limited space prevented Howard Garfinkel and I from including many of the lectures we wanted in the book. Nor were we able to completely capture the impact of the speakers as they taught and motivated their audience. Sometimes you just "had to be there" to get the full impact. Still, we have tried to capture the true spirit of the men and their messages in edited form.

We hope that being able to "sit in" on these lectures will benefit all readers, regardless of their endeavors.

ED SCHILLING

Contents

Dedication

*"It cannot touch my mind, it cannot touch my heart,
it cannot touch my soul."*

Jim Valvano, ESPY Awards, March 4, 1993

When you speak about Jim Valvano, you speak about one of the most passionate men I've ever met. He epitomized what was truly indicative of being a beautiful person. He brought a smile to the face of everyone he touched, because he owned the magical gift of a master communicator. He lit up every room he entered with his witty personality and genuine love for people. In battling his dreaded cancer, he captured the affection of the nation with his courage and tenacity.

Jim Valvano embodied what is good about people. He provided inspiration for so many, not for cutting down the nets in 1983 with his overachieving North Carolina State team, but for standing tall in meeting adversity head-on. He lit the way in showing others that you must never stop battling, never stop fighting, when faced with a crisis. As Jimmy Vee said, "Don't give up! You must never, ever give up!"

I've always felt that Jim Valvano could have been a star in anything he attempted, so it certainly didn't surprise me that he became an instant superstar in television. He was more than just a PTP'er, a prime-time performer, as a teacher, coach, hoop analyst and entertainer — he was All-Rolls Royce, a solid-gold human being!

I loved him, his family and friends loved him, the world of basketball loved him ... America loved him!

DICK VITALE

Jim Valvano first captured the collective heart of the nation as a coach at North Carolina State, where his underdog team won an unforgettable national championship in 1983. He did it again in a far more important struggle, his courageous battle against cancer. Valvano lost that fight in 1993, but he was an inspiration to people all over the country because of his relentless spirit and optimism. He gave this lecture as an unknown college coach at Iona in 1976. He had big dreams then, and he made them come true. Looking back, it's no wonder.

★ Jim Valvano

I'll tell you something fellas, I am super-psyched. I am ready to roll. I love kids. Basically, I am out of my mind. Starting today is my 14th straight day of camp. I do 72 camps. I have eaten camp food for 14 straight days now — I am going to crap my way from here through the midwest, but I love it. I can't stop. I am an addict. I wake up in the morning and I can't wait to go to work.

How about your fathers? Any of your fathers salesmen? No? Do any of your fathers work at all? Your father sells ink? Now there's a great job. No, that is important. What if there was no ink, we couldn't sign any players. Your dad probably wakes up in the morning and says, "Hey, somebody get me a pen, quick, I got to sell some ink!" He can't wait to get to work and sell more ink, right? No, he probably gets up and says, "Holy crap, it's Monday and I've got five days to sell that damn ink — red ink, blue ink, black ink." He probably hates it, right?

Basketball people love what they are doing. I got up this morning all psyched up to speak and then Garf gives me a great introduction. I come out here, and what do I see? From this angle I see 200 crotch shots. It's true — that guy has a jock on, that guy has a rash, that guy doesn't need a jock. That's super, Garf has everybody here showing me their jewels.

I am going to start a Five-Star tradition today: standing ovations. I run a camp and nobody walks through my door and doesn't receive a standing ovation. Now I know you are probably saying, "Who wants to give this guy a standing ovation?" I am a nobody, I agree with you. Garf is giving me my intro and says, " . . . from Iona college." And this guy over here is saying, "This guy Valvano owns his own college? At his age!" You have never heard of me or my school.

You are going to have some heavy hitters coming this week — Digger Phelps, Hubie Brown, the greatest, is going to be here, guys that speak all over the place. Hubie Brown, the great coach of the Atlanta Hawks, is going to walk on to this court, spend an hour-and-a-half with you and you guys are going to give him 200 crotch shots. He makes 80 billion dollars a year and he has to look at your jewels. Some guys see your jewels and aren't going to be quite as psyched.

What I want, for your sake, is to greet them with a standing ovation. Here, let's try it. I'm going to introduce this guy. What is your name? Joel Blumberg. Ok, we are going to give Joel a standing O after I introduce him.

"Making his Five-Star debut, all the way from New Jersey, the one, the only, Joel Blumberg!" (The campers stand and cheer.) Holy crap, Joel. Now a guy comes in here and gets this standing ovation and reception and he's going to think that this is a classy camp. You know what, he'll do a better job for you.

So what am I really talking about? I'm talking about one word — enthusiasm. That's what I want, enthusiasm. Ralph Waldo Emerson. Who'd he play for? No, he was a writer, he said something that I want you to keep in mind throughout the whole camp. It was, "Nothing great has ever been accomplished without enthusiasm." I want to accomplish great things, and I am sure you guys want to as well. So you got to be psyched about it.

So you start right now, you start by being enthusiastic. Why should you be enthusiastic? Well, to begin with, the guy coming out here to give his lecture is going to do a better job. No. 2, what did it cost to come here, $140 smackers? Wow! I'm from Queens, New York, and, I'll tell you, $140 in Queens could buy you four broads for the weekend. Instead of spending your money on something like that, you choose to come here. So why sit on your butt?

What I want to do here is motivate you. And I want you to motivate me by giving me some feedback. You'll have a super hour-and-a-half because we are all going to be psyched. Come on up here, son. What is your name? Bill Most, from Millburn, New Jersey. Today is the most important day in Bill Most's life, because today is the day that Bill Most decides to become enthusiastic. Ralph Waldo says you can accomplish great things. Bill Most comes here and he is psyched out of his mind. Ohh, does Bill have a week of camp. Garf gives him a 5+ in his scouting service. Garf says, "Bill Most, the most on toast." Yes, Bill, yes! They love him, big-time potential. What school do you want to go to Bill?

"Virginia."

Now the coach of Virginia picks up the H.S.B.I. scouting report and reads about Bill Most, the most on toast, and offers you a full ride. You use the pen from the ink man in the back and sign to play at Virginia, because of what you did here at Five-Star. Bill goes to Virginia, has a great career and the agents are recruiting him. What team in the NBA do you want to play for Bill?

"The New York Knicks."

Bill! They need you, Bill. He opens his own bar on the east side, they love him in New York. Bill Most marries the playmate of the year. Look at him, the pimples are clearing up already. Bill's excited already, look at him. Bill goes on and has a great life, all because he got excited Monday.

Now, what if Bill was a stiff and didn't want to get up like some of the guys I saw a few minutes ago? So, Bill didn't get excited here and he goes back to Millburn and his face is covered with acne by then. You could squeeze Bill's neck and pus would come out of his hands. Bill marries some fat, ugly broad from Millburn that has a mustache, hair on her legs, under her arm pits, and, oh, does she smell. Unbelievable!

Which would you rather have, Bill? This whole thing sounds silly, but I'm telling you that you can accomplish great things if you have enthusiasm.

The second thing that you need to have is attitude. If Mr. Garfinkel puts on his report that you have a bad attitude, you are done. Maybe more important than ability is your attitude. There are only two kinds of people in the world — big-timers and rats. There are big-time campers, there are big-time lecturers, there are big-time coaches, there are big-time pros and then there are rats. That's all there are. The big-timers, you see 'em at camp, they've got their clippings under their arms. There are big-time coaches too, they come up and say, "Well, I just got back from the coast and I just signed a multi-million dollar deal. So if you want to know what it is like to coach in the bigs ... "

Big-time campers have one word in their vocabulary; it starts with an "S" and ends with a "K" and has two letters in the middle. Suck, that's it. You get your assignment after the lecture and you're walking away and you ask the big-time camper what he thought and he answers, "I thought it sucked." You ask him after the first day what he thinks of his coach and he says, "He sucks." You ask him about that guy over there who's supposed to be an All-American and he says, "I think he sucks."

The worst thing in the world are big-time pros. The big-time pro shows up to give a lecture and he walks out and sits on the ball and says, "Any questions? Any of you guys want to know how great it is to be in the NBA?" Some kid asks who the best guard is, and he says, "Ha, you are lookin' at him." Then he says, "You guys want to see some ballhandling? O.K. this half of the camp come out and guard me."

Another thing about big-time pros is that they never give names. They call guys things like, "Hey, Blue Socks, come here." Then the big-time pro will say, "O.K., here's a good post move for you young guys out there. Pump fake like this, and then bam, dunk the crap out of the ball, like this. Here's the next one, pump fake here, then reverse dunk it, like this. Got it? Here Blue Socks, you do it." Then the camp laughs at Blue Socks and he says that's why he's a pro.

What you need are rats! You need rats. We need rat campers. Guys that love to be at camp. You are all going to have the runs, you know that don't you? Today was the best meal you will have all week. Rat campers get up out of bed and they get in a defensive stance and start shuffling their feet in a defensive stance to breakfast. They over-play the potatoes. Lunch? Who says you got to eat lunch? A rat camper goes out and guards a tree for awhile! That's what we want — we want rat campers.

Rat campers do one thing, they take the offensive foul. They take the charge. A rat camper will take a charge. A rat camper will go home and sneak up on his little sister and boom, take a charge when she walks out of her bedroom. I fouled my wife out of the house last week; she's gone. Build up and take the charge from your father when you think you're ready. My players are up to taking charges from small foreign cars right now. Yeah, step in on a Volvo someday.

I'm giving two awards here at Five-Star. You have to decide, one is the Super Rat award, which goes to the guy who takes the most charges. A Super Rat is a rat taking a charge. And the other award is the Challenge. Here's a Five-Star challenge: somebody, please take a charge on Mr. Garfinkel. Yes, one guy, when Garf is running around camp saying, "Yes, he's a 3 +, he's a 2 +," somebody step in and take a charge from Mr. G. I got a shirt for that guy. When I'm out traveling around, I want to hear that somebody took a charge on Garf.

I'm a little strange, as you have probably already figured out, and I carry with me all summer a stuffed rat. Now my stuffed Super Rat, who is making his Five-Star debut, was playing a pick-up game in the Bronx one day and he stepped in and took a charge from a German Shepherd. Tough game. My Super Rat met his death that day, and this is his spirit with us now. What I want now is a Five-Star standing ovation for the Super Rat. (The kids stand and cheer.)

They say I'm crazy, but I just got 200 guys to stand up and cheer for a dead, stuffed rat. Think about that. See, when I first got out here, you wouldn't even stand up and cheer for me. Twenty minutes later we are up cheering for a dead, stuffed rat. That's fantastic, that's what I'm talking about — enthusiasm.

You can accomplish great things with two aspects here at camp right now. No. 1, get psyched up and fired up. No. 2, have the proper attitude. I can look around right now and point out some guys who are big-dealing me. Rubbing their eyes and leaning back ... bull crap, we don't need them here and we don't need them in basketball. They won't amount to anything. I want people who want to accomplish great things. Nobody accomplishes anything when they start thinking they are better than somebody else. As soon as you start thinking you're bigger than somebody else you are in big trouble.

I want you to be enthusiastic and I want you to be a rat. You talk about wanting to be a pro, do you know how hard it is to be a pro? Let me give you some statistics. Last year 18,000 college basketball players played and 175 were drafted and maybe two will make each team. That's 36 guys, that's one-half of one percent of the guys that played college basketball who end up playing in the pros. A lot of guys think that's where they are going. "NBA Jack, that's where I'm going."

If it is so tough to make it, then why should you shoot for it at all? There was a recent study that showed that 99 percent of all people use less than one percent of their ability. Coaches say they have guys that give 110 percent. I say they're full of crap. I want guys to give me five percent. If you have the enthusiasm and the proper attitude, then you can reach your potential. Is that the one-half of one percent? I don't know, maybe it is.

Talk about potential. Have you guys ever heard of Johnny Weismuller? He's the Tarzan guy. He held 59 United States swimming records, the most ever held by one person. They said that no one would ever break his records. You know who broke his records? Everybody says Mark Spitz. You know who broke Weismuller's records? Now 13-year-old girls swim faster than he ever swam in his life. Can you imagine him with Jane in his arm and Cheetah, backstrokin', and he gets out of the water and some guy comes up and says that some 13-year-old broad is going to swim faster than him. Yeah, right — the guy would have gotten hit in the head with a coconut, he'd have been dead.

What's your potential? You know what I think? I think your potential is unlimited. Your potential is unlimited with the proper attitude, the desire to be a rat and to be enthusiastic. Why should you do it, why you should go for it? I'm going to tell you a story about three great men. Teddy Roosevelt, a former President, said in a thing called The Battle of Life, "The credit belongs to the man in the arena. The credit belongs to the man who has the sweat, who tries to do the deed, who fails, gets up and tries again, who in the end knows the triumph of high achievement."

Richard Nixon said, "You cannot imagine how great it is to be on the highest mountain unless you have been to the deepest valley." For nine years I have been in the valley of coaching, working to someday get to the highest mountain. I reached the top of the mountain once as a player at Rutgers, as a walk-on; I paid my way. The biggest thrill of my life would have been to play in Madison Square Garden. My freshman year, we didn't make it. My sophomore year, we didn't make it. My junior year, we didn't make it. My senior year, we finally made it to the NIT. My freshman year, I rode the pine, I didn't get into any games. You know how coaches are, they walk down and tell you, "Get into the game, get into the game, cheer for your teammates. C'mon, get into the game!" And I'm sitting there thinking, I'd love to get into the game, but I can't get into the game; I'm sitting here. Coach is telling me to cheer and I'm clapping and saying, "I hope one of my teammates breaks his leg so I can get into the game."

So it is finally my senior year and we are in the NIT, and we play Utah State in the first round and we beat their butts. Then we beat New Mexico. Then we play a team that had a guy on it named Walt Frazier in the 9 o'clock game in Madison Square Garden. For a guy from the city, this is the top of the mountain. It is 9 o'clock and I'm sitting on the bench. It is the 9 o'clock game, not the 7 o'clock game, and all the broads have minks on, oh yeah. I am sitting there, getting ready to be introduced. My whole life has been waiting to go from the bench to the middle of the court. The guy is announcing, "And now, starting at guard for Rutgers, at 6 foot 4" — I was a lot bigger then — "brown hair, blue eyes, good looking son-of-a-gun, Jim Valvano." Yes! I had waited my whole life for this, to go from the bench to the middle of the court. I had waited 19 years of my life for this moment. Now, how am I going to get out there? Here is what you have to do: first, you have to stay there awhile, so the fans are saying, "Where is he?" Then you have to go for the reverse behind-the-back hand slap.

I want you to reach the top of your mountain someday, and I want you to enjoy it. I have only gotten there one time, so far, but I want to go there again.

We talked about some silly stuff, but we also talked about being enthusiastic. We talked about being a rat. We talked about reaching the top of your mountain.

Now I want to talk some hoops. The real world of basketball. What do you have to do to reach the top of the mountain in the game of basketball? Win. You have got to win. Everybody say it. "Win!" You bet, you have got to win. Don't ever forget it. If anybody ever comes out here and says that winning isn't important, then they're nuts. Don't believe them, winning is important. There are no awards for losing in the real world. The ideal world, maybe.

What do coaches say when they talk to each other before the game? They say, "Hey, how's it going? Saw your team play the other day, you looked good. How's the wife and family? Good, glad to hear it. Good luck tonight." Do you think the coach really means that? What the coach would really want to say is, "I hope we beat your ass." When you shake hands before the tip with the other players, what do you say? "Good luck, have a good game." What do you want, "Hey, good luck, I hope you score 40 tonight and by the way, my girl is up there in the stands, you can have her later too." No way! What you really feel is that you will kick his ass if you get the chance.

That's the real world. Winning is important. The academic people will say that it is just important to participate. Yeah, right. If you take a chemistry test 10 times and you flunk it 10 times and go home and say, "Dad, I participated," what will he say? Go tell your teacher that and she will say that you are stupid. They will label you stupid.

Labels are important in society. However, the label that you do not want in basketball is "loser." Twenty-six times a year, you step out on the court and find out what you are made of — you do not want to lose. Winning is important.

Now, to get to win you have got to work. Bob Richards, who was the world champion pole vaulter, says that he worked 52,000 hours on pole vaulting. You know how long that is? That's like seven years. What I think you need is a summer program that involves all phases of the game: dribbling, passing, shooting, rebounding, defending, running, and moving without the ball. The workout should last about an hour-and-a-half.

If you want to reach the top of your mountain, then you better be ready to work for it. I was a big-timer, I was the assistant coach of University of Connecticut. I had all the suits and that stuff that big-time assistants had. One day we received a letter from a kid nine years old and he asked for the game ball signed by all the players. We didn't have time for that. We sent him a picture, didn't have time for the ball thing. Got another letter saying to please send him a game ball. Ahh, we didn't have time to send him a signed game ball, so we sent him another picture.

The young man was very ill, he was about to have open heart surgery. Our team eventually went to see that kid and we found out that the kid had been in bed for four years. Yes, four years! But we got guys here getting tired during an hour lecture. For four years, that kid did not miss listening to a single game on the radio. He thought our players and coaches were special.

After seeing him, we dedicated our last game to him. It was a big rivalry against Rhode Island, a big game. We weren't a great team that year, but we went out for that game and played with great enthusiasm — we played with our hearts! But we went out and we lost. I saw a 45-year-old man, the head coach, cry. I saw 15 players cry. We felt we had let the kid down. We went to the hospital and presented him with a signed ball. Now at UConn they have an award named after that young man, given to the player who is like the rat that we have talked about.

I wish this story had a happy ending and the kid came back and won a college scholarship, but I don't. The kid had open heart surgery and about a month later he died. Nine years old and he died! After he died the parents wrote our team a letter that I have memorized. I would like to share it with you, in it is everything I have talked about.

The mother said, "Please express our deepest appreciation to the members of the basketball team for their kindness to our son Jimmy. You can't imagine how much it meant for him to have the ball and the pictures. The ball never left his side from the moment he received it, he even slept with it. Please tell the team that because of them, they made the last week of a little boy's life a happy one. They will have a place in our hearts forever." I'll say the last line again: "Because of them" — people like you, coaches like me, because of us — "they made the last week of a little boy's life a happy one."

Fellas, that's why I go to camp, that's why I talked at the beginning about not being a big-timer but instead being a rat. Because I believe that the ideals of basketball combined with the realities of basketball can be one of the most meaningful experiences you will ever have. Somebody out there thinks that somebody in here is somebody special. The way you lead your life is going to affect somebody else. I'm here to say that I would like all of you here to reach the top of that mountain and I would like somewhere along the line for you to reach out and touch someone's life. So that someone can say that: "*. . . made the last week of someone's life a happy one.*" That's what it is about, that's what the game is about, showing people that you care. That's why I told you about standing ovations. Show people you care. That's why I don't want you to be a big-timer, I want you to be a rat. Do something meaningful.

I know that this is the one of the best camps in the world, if not the best. So, I'm challenging you to have a one heck of a great week. Don't be a big-timer; show all the lecturers that you care and go back to your school and contribute in some way. My team won 10 games last year; that's a failure, right? Wrong, we ran one of the best programs in the country. My team visited hospitals, visited the home for the mentally retarded, and adopted a child through the Big Brothers program. My players gave me some of their meal money for a young man in Bedford Stuy.

Hey, that's what I want you to take away from here; that you can be whatever you want to be. Your talent and potential is unlimited. Lead your life in a way as to give something back. If you do that, you will be the biggest success you could possibly be. I said when I came here that I love coming to camps, and I do. And I love the people out here. I wish you all the best week of basketball that you have ever had, and hope that you all reach the top of your mountain.

An overachiever as a player at Miami of Ohio, Ed Schilling has continued in that manner as a high school coach in Indiana. He turned around the program at Western Boone, breaking the school record for wins in his third season, and is now taking on an even greater challenge at Logansport in one of the country's most competitive conferences. He's already gained widespread recognition for his coaching ability, as evidenced by his selection as a head coach in the McDonald's Capital Classic All-American game. This young coach appears destined for a great career.

★ Ed Schilling

It is an honor to speak with you today, because it wasn't long ago that I sat right where you are sitting now. I was a camper here as a rising junior and a senior. As I speak with you today, understand that I know that I don't have all the answers. I learn new things every day.

In fact, I learn the most from people like you. You teach and reinforce ideas about competitiveness and persistence that keep me going during the tough times. I see you giving it everything you have in statlons and then at the individual instructions and that fires me up to reach down and teach what I know about the game a little bit better and with more intensity and enthusiasm. I don't know it all, I promise you that, but at the same time I am going to work my butt off to give you some things that will allow you to become more successful with the game of basketball.

To begin with, you need to set some personal goals. Now I know from coaching my high school teams that most of the time we do not create goals that are specific enough to challenge us into dramatic improvement. Goals need to be broken down into three basic categories — long term, intermediate, and short term.

The most important of these is the long term goal. I really believe that if you are going to come close to reaching your potential, you have to have a lofty long term goal. This goal must be, in reality, more than a goal, it must be a dream — a goal with so much feeling that when you put your head on your pillow at night the image of where you want to go evolves into a crystal clear picture. That dream, that long term goal, is different for everybody. My goal was to play in the

NCAA tournament on national television in the heat of March Madness. Your goal may be to play in the NBA or to run out for the starting line-up on your high school team. The dream is different for everybody, and you don't have to share the dream with anybody. When I shared my dream with others when I was a 5-7, 120-pound freshman in high school, they laughed at me. Regardless of what other people say if you share your goal with them, your dream must remain a motivational force that is reviewed daily.

Next, you need to formulate your intermediate goals. Where do you want to be in six months? What do you want to be able to do when school starts in the fall? This intermediate goal will keep you going when you have short term setbacks and your dream seems so far away. This intermediate goal setting should be done through the season as well. While the long term goal may seem quite unattainable at times, the intermediate goal should be challenging, but still attainable. The intermediate goal should also be measurable — something that can be measured and charted.

The last part of this plan is the setting of day-to-day goals. Every time you step onto the basketball court, you need to have something specific for which to work. If you were to meet on the park with some friends to play basketball and you got there and there were no goals on the backboards, the game would lose its excitement after awhile. The same is true with your individual game — you need to have goals to make the game fun and challenging. Don't get me wrong, you can still do a lot of positive things in this game without the stuff I'm telling you, but if you are a competitor, which most successful athletes are, then you perform best when you have a specific challenge.

The off-season workout that I am going to show you allows for you to have daily goals, and from those daily goals you can formulate your intermediate goals with your dream shining down throughout. I achieved a lot of success in the game of basketball and outside of basketball due to my work ethic. This inner work ethic began to explode when I started dedicating myself toward my daily workout program. If you make the decision to commit to a workout program, you should also get a notebook to record your results. When you write down how many shots you made out of how many, and how many free throws you made out of how many you took, you then create a standard to which you can measure your improvements or digressions. If you don't write your results down, then you'll never really know how much you have improved.

When I was in high school and college, I had a red notebook where I recorded all my individual workouts. I can tell you how many free throws I took and made on any given day from 1984 through 1987. I can also tell you the ballhandling drills that I did. I found that when I started recording my workouts, I felt the self inflicted pressure to do them daily and I also found I began to strive for excellence on each drill because I knew what I did the day before and I wanted to do better. This exercise in striving for excellence will carry over into all areas of your life. The will to improve isn't shut on and off like a water faucet, it flows from one area of your life to another.

Let's get into the workout. First, you need to understand that when you make the decision to improve your game through the workout I am going to show you, you must go through it with game speed intensity on each drill and activity. If you don't practice at game speed and intensity, then you will not be able to perform in the game situation because the situation will be foreign if you haven't practiced at that intensity. I believe in the efficiency of time. As the saying goes, it's quality, not quantity. I used to spend six and seven hours playing ball a day, but when I started spending less time but with greater intensity, that is when I saw the most results. So, when you cross the line to do the workout, make up your mind to give it your all. No breaks, and no social time. For 50 minutes or so you focus on making your game better.

We start the workout with 50 consecutive jump rope turns on the right leg. If you mess up on 49, you start over. Next, you complete 50 consecutive jumps on the left foot. Then you jump 100 times on both feet without a mistake. The jump rope is one of the best friends to an athlete, and an especially good friend to a big man. This quick routine will develop foot quickness, agility and jumping quickness while serving as a warmup exercise as well.

Now we get a basketball. We begin with the Mikan Drill — continuous left- and right-hand hooks facing the backboard, jumping off the opposite leg that you are shooting with. Be sure to bank the shot in and jump as high as possible on each shot. Make 10 shots with each hand, alternating hands on each shot.

Next, execute the Mikan Drill, but this time have your back to the backboard. This is very much like a reverse layup. Make 10 with each hand again, just like you did facing the goal.

The last part of the Mikan Drill section is to do what we call the miscellaneous Mikan. You add fakes and spins and basically any move that you can think of under the basket. Make 20 of these shots. The theory regarding this is to be comfortable finishing any potential shot around the goal, so that if you catch a pass and get to the basket you will have the confidence that you can make just about any shot that could possibly present itself.

After you make your last shot of the Mikan section, go directly to the free throw line and *make* — not shoot — five free throws. Then you record in your notebook the number of shots it took you to make five free throws and check off the three parts of the Mikan section.

Now we move on to the ballhandling portion. You need to do two of these potential four ballhandling drills each time you do the workout. The first drill you might choose to do is called the Zig-Zag Drill. On this drill you start at the corner where the end line and side line intersect and zig-zag down the court driving at the free throw (elbow) lane and line intersection, then executing a dribble move — such as a crossover, behind the back, between the legs or spin move — then you explode to the halfcourt side line intersection where you execute a dribble move. You do this down the court, then across the end line to the end line and side line intersection, where you do the same thing, zig-zagging down the court on that side. Execute two complete laps working on a dribble move at each point.

The second drill you might do is the Up Two, Back Two Drill. You will do two sets, 60 seconds each. You begin by dribbling up two dribbles, then you execute two pull-back dribbles with the ball even with and behind the back leg, sliding backward so that the ball is protected. After the two backward dribbles, you snap a cross-over dribble below the knee and go forward with two dribbles. After two dribbles up, you again do two pull-back dribbles, a cross-over dribble and so on. You perform this continually for 60 seconds. Take two free throws for a short rest period, then do another 60-second set of Up Two, Back Two.

The third drill is called Kill the Grass. In an area about the size of the jump ball circle, you should execute as many dribble moves as possible in 60 seconds. It is called Kill the Grass because if there were grass growing in the area you would attempt to kill all of it with the bouncing ball. Therefore, you need to imagine going by a defender with a dribble move. This drill allows you to get fancy while doing a variety of dribble drills and moving about the entire circle. You go for 60 seconds, then shoot two free throws, then do another 60-second set.

The fourth drill is called the Chill Drill. You start on the end line-side line intersection with the ball in the right hand. You go up the side line executing the inside-out dribble move. At the halfcourt-side line intersection you execute a spin dribble, switching the ball to the left hand. Continue across the halfcourt line until the nearest point of the jump ball circle; at this point you perform a pull back cross-over. This is done by taking two dribbles backward and then executing a cross-over dribble.

Now, proceed as fast as possible to the other side of the jump ball circle on the halfcourt line; there you perform a "half-a-whirl," or fake reverse. Pushing off the right foot as you come out of the fake reverse, you explode to the halfcourt-side line intersection where you perform a behind-the-back dribble. The ball goes from the right hand to the left. Proceed to the elbow of the free throw lane dribbling with the left hand. At that point you do a stutter step cross-over dribble and extend to the basket with one dribble and lay the ball in the basket.

Perform the Chill Drill three times, starting with the ball in the right hand on the right side, and then three times starting with the ball in the left hand on the left side.

Choose two of these four drills with each workout. Be sure to vary them. After you do the ballhandling drills, go directly to the free throw line and make five free throws. Record how many free throws it took you to make five. Also, record which ballhandling drills you did.

The next section of the workout is post moves. It is important to be able to score from the post, because in most offenses everybody posts up at some point. If the man guarding you is in foul trouble or if you have a size advantage, you can take him to the block and work on him if you have a game down low. The way we work on the post move is to choose three of the seven post moves, then go from block to block and make five shots from each block using one post move. After you have made 10 moves and shots, go to the next post move.

You may choose three of the following:

Drop step baseline

Drop step middle

Fake middle, drop step baseline

Fake baseline, drop step to the middle

Quick spin either way

Sikma

Up and under

After you have completed 10 successful shots for each post move, go to the free throw line and make five free throws. Record the results and the post moves that you worked on.

Next, move on to the shooting portion of the workout. I don't believe in starting out with 20-foot jumpers, so the first thing we do is make 15 "form jumpers." We concentrate on the form of the shot, starting in close to the basket and moving out with each shot. After you make 15 form jumpers, go to the free throw line and make 10 free throws.

After recording the free throws, we go to game situation shooting. We are going to make 20 jump shots and we will record the number taken to make 20. I am into making shots, not simply taking shots. The first shot we are going to shoot is as if we are coming off a screen. We simulate this by spinning the ball out and running out to catch it just like you would if you were coming off a screen. Have your butt down and hands in the ready position, pick the ball up and shoot the jumper. After releasing the jumper, follow your shot and spin it out to another position on the floor; repeat this until you have made 20 shots. Keep track of how many shots it takes you to make 20. After making the 20th jumper, go to the free throw line and make 10 free throws, then record both the jumpers and the free throws.

The next shot to work on is to shot fake, take one dribble and then shoot a jumper. We do this in the same manner as the shot coming off a screen, except now we catch the ball, shot fake, dribble and shoot. Make 20 jumpers and 10 free throws, then record the number of attempts needed for both.

After the shot fake, we go on to the next move. Spin the ball out as before, catch it and square to the basket, then fake right and take a long, strong dribble to the left and shoot the jumper. Make 20 of these and 10 free throws and record the attempts needed.

Our next move is to fake left and go right. Make 20 fake-left-and go-right jumpers and 10 free throws and write down the total attempts.

Next, we execute a one-on-one move after the spin out and square up. This move can be a rocker step, a shot fake, a quick move off a jab step and so on; after the move, shoot the pull-up jumper. As usual, hit 20 shots and 10 free throws and then record them.

The last move is any one-on-one move to a layup. Make 20 of these moves and finish — be sure not to travel — and then shoot 10 free throws and record both.

In this workout you jump rope, work on Mikan Drill hooks and layups, ballhandling, post moves, and a variety of game situation shooting. I cannot guarantee you that this workout will make you achieve your long term goal, but I can guarantee you that it will improve your game. When you do this workout at game speed and intensity, you will make positive strides toward achieving your dream.

It isn't easy to dedicate yourself to something, and there will be countless obstacles in your way. When I was a rising sophomore in high school, I decided that I wanted to play college basketball and play

It isn't easy to dedicate yourself to something, and there will be countless obstacles in your way. When I was a rising sophomore in high school, I decided that I wanted to play college basketball and play on national television during the NCAA tournament in March. So I worked on my game for five and six hours a day, seven days a week.

I remember as clearly as if it were yesterday, it was a Saturday night and I was shooting on my basket in our yard. I had it worked out so that the goal was lit up a little with the street light and a makeshift spotlight. Our house was on a busy road and some of the guys in my grade drove by and yelled through the open car window some profanities and asked, "Don't you have anything better to do than to play basketball by yourself?" They proceeded to throw some beer bottles near my court as they peeled out and drove off.

Events like that one are tough to handle when you are in high school. Also, some of my friends who used to play a lot of basketball were getting into other things, and they no longer wanted to spend the majority of their day hooping. Consequently, I found I was pretty much alone in my attempt to achieve my dream.

However, it was a few years later in March that the public address announcer said, "Starting at guard, from Lebanon, Indiana, 6-2, Ed Schilling!" As we lined up for the jump ball against Maryland and the likes of Len Bias, I briefly remembered the comments of those who said I couldn't make it at the college level, and further back to when the guys threw the beer bottles on my court and asked if I didn't have something better to do than play with myself. It was during that game, which was shown on ESPN, that I decided that all the work, the loneliness and sacrifice was worth it.

The interesting part of this story is that when I went back to the town where I received those vicious comments, the first guys to run up to me and shake my hand and tell me that they were cheering for me in the NCAA tournament and how great it was to see one of "their boys" playing on television were the guys who had made those comments.

Why do I tell you this story? Because you need to know that it is going to be tough improving your game, especially if you are physically limited like I was. Your peers may make fun of you, your friends might find other interests, and still others may tempt you with drugs and alcohol, but if you really want to make your dream become a reality, then you can't be discouraged from setting and working to achieve your short term, intermediate, and long term goals. One of the best ways you can make progress in the game is to dedicate yourself to an individual workout.

Good luck!

Xavier coach Pete Gillen describes himself as ``just a singles hitter in this home run life.'' Then again, Pete Rose, another Cincinnati-based sports figure, did all right as a singles hitter. Gillen has lifted Xavier, a small private school, to the level of the giants. He has won 73 percent of his games in eight seasons, and has been named the conference's Coach of the Year four times. His teams have competed in the NCAA Tournament in all but one of his seasons, advancing to the Sweet Sixteen in 1990. And don't forget this vital statistic: every senior who has played for him has received his degree.

★ Pete Gillen

The great thing about basketball is that there are many ways to do things, and many ways to be successful. The things that I am going to talk about are not the only way to play the game. These ideas and techniques have been good to us over the last few years and I hope thay they can help you in some way.

My goal today is to help everyone here with at least one thought or concept or drill that you can use to help make your team better next season. I am going to talk to you about five basic things: 1. The mental part of the inside game; 2. Techniques on how to get the ball inside; 3. Drills on how to get the ball inside; 4. Offensive concepts in developing an inside game; 5. Individual development of the inside game.

I feel that 80 percentof the game today is mental. We really stress with our players at Xavier that we want them to get the ball inside as much as they can. If the defense really sags, then they should not hesitate to shoot their jump shot. But, we want them to look inside first.

Whatever your coach feels is very important, you should try to do that thing very well. With me, it is important to get the ball inside and those players on my team who execute this the best usually play the most.

Basketball is a lot like a game of chess. In chess, if you can get your opponent's big pieces — like the queen, the rook, and the knight — off the board, you will win the game. The same thing holds true in basketball. If you get the ball inside you will draw a lot of fouls, and the opposing coach will have to take his big men off the court because of foul trouble. When the other team's big men are out of the game, then you have a great chance to win the game and your potential to play well individually increases greatly.

I believe that the toughest place to guard someone in the game of basketball is in the low post area, because if you make one mistake on defense and the offensive player knows how to play, the offensive player will get a great percentage shot or he will get fouled.

Basketball is a game of angles and percentages. We must know the best angles to get the ball inside. This will depend on where the defense is playing us in the low post area. The best percentage shots are usually the ones in the low post area.

The second major point I would like to share with you is the techniques on how to get the ball inside. I have seven basic ideas for the low post player.

No. 1, start on the opposite side of the floor from where you want to post up. A weak side cut is very difficult to defend. You can fake high and go low by jamming off your right foot in a V-cut move. Or you can fake low to go high. Here you would come up a little higher in the post area. I would then jam off my left foot in a V-cut move.

No. 2, come to a jump stop on the first hash mark above the box. You want to land with a jump stop because you can use either foot as your pivot foot. You want to land on the first hash mark above the box and then if you turn baseline, you still have a good angle to shoot the ball off the backboard. If you get the ball on the box and then turn baseline, you will have to shoot the ball straight in. I believe this six- to eight-foot shot is very difficult. We encourage our players to use the backboard every chance they get in the low post area.

The third point is to take up a lot of room, really bend your knees, and locate the defense. After you make contact with your defender, you should try to keep contact with him. Try to keep your defensive man "locked" in one spot so it is easier for the passer to get you the ball inside. Your feet should be spread a little wider than the width of your shoulders. We don't want the offensive post player to do the splits, but we want him to take up as much room down there as he can and still be comfortable.

Next, give a target hand away from your defensive man. It is very important that the feeder or passer has an exact spot to throw to. A catcher in baseball gives the pitcher a target and a spot to hit. The low post player must also give the passer a target to hit. The low post player should really extend his hand to give a big target to the passer. He can extend his hand either high or low, wherever he wishes.

The fifth idea is to break the defender's arm up or break it down. By this we mean we are going to lift up or lean on and push down the defender's forward arm, the one that is closest to the passer. We break the defender's arm up by simply putting our arm underneath the defensive man's arm at his elbow and lifting our arm up three inches. This locks the defender's front arm and prevents him from deflecting the pass as it comes into the low post. We break the defender's arm down by putting our arm over his forward arm at the elbow area and just bring our arm down three inches. This also locks the defender's arm and stops him from intercepting or deflecting the pass into the pivot. This is a perfectly legal maneuver, and we are not pushing off or "clearing out" or elbowing our defender in any way. We want to keep our defender in this locked position for as long as possible until the ball is almost in our hands.

Point No. 6 is to reach your arms out and come to meet the pass. Basketball, like baseball, is often a game of inches. The low post man should not stand there with his hands at his sides and wait for the ball to come to him. He should reach out to receive the ball. He might even have to take a step with one foot toward the ball if he feels he is in danger, or he thinks the pass could be stolen or deflected. If he does this, he is establishing a pivot foot and he cuts down on the variety of things he can do in the low post area. But the most important thing is to catch the ball, and if he has to take a step to meet the pass, then he should do so. The low post player should look the ball into his hands with his eyes. You catch the ball with your eyes as well as your hands. If you don't believe me, try catching a post pass with your eyes closed.

The last point in this area of post play is very underrated in today's game, and it is to not be afraid to pass the ball back outside when you get the ball in the low post area. Most players when they get the ball in the pivot area just hold on to it and shoot it at all costs. Very often the low post player is double- or triple-teamed, and he can't do a thing with the ball. Don't try to force things in the low post area. By kicking the ball back outside, the low post man will often get the ball right back again for an easy shot because the defender many times relaxes when the ball is passed out of the post.

These seven points are the basics for the low post player, but these ideas are useless if the ball cannot be effectively entered to him. So we need to know how to get the ball into the post. Here are the seven keys to getting the ball to the teammate posting up.

No. 1, the passer must have the confidence and guts to throw the ball into the low post. Many times a perimeter player might see a man free in the low post area, but he is afraid to throw the ball in there. He is afraid that the ball might be deflected or stolen. He is afraid of the verbal abuse he might get from his coach if he makes a mistake. Rather than take a chance, he plays it safe and passes to someone else on the perimeter.

No. 2, the passer or feeder should see how and where the defense is playing the man in the low post. He should see if the defense is fronting the low post or not. He should see if the defense is playing three-quarters on the baseline side. He should see if the defense is playing behind the low post man. The passer should see if the defense varies in the low post area, or if they always guard you the same way. By knowing how the defense is playing your post-up man, this will tell you how you can best feed the man in the pivot.

Next, you must know and understand your angles. If the defense is playing the low post man three-quarters on the high side, take the ball toward the corner and throw a baseline bounce pass. Most of the time the man on defense in the low post area will play three-quarters on the high side. If the man on defense is playing three-quarters on the baseline side, take the ball toward the foul line area and throw a bounce pass inside. If the defense is completely fronting the man in the low post, the man on offense should inch his way up the lane toward the foul line. By doing this he is also bringing the defense up the lane. Then as we get more room between the two players and the baseline, the passer has a better angle to throw a lob pass. The passer lobs the ball and aims for the bottom corner of the backboard right at the edge. The player on offense now seals off the defender and locks him there until the ball is directly over his head on the lob pass. Then the offensive player rolls his hips and gives the defensive player a little bump with his hips to get the defender off balance. Then the offensive player releases his pressure and goes for the lob pass and lays the ball in. Try not to let the defense front you, but if you can't get free from being fronted, rely on this set up for the lob pass.

If the defender always plays behind in the low post, get the ball in the post as often as possible. If you are not sure how the defense is playing the low post man, then take the ball toward the baseline. Also, take the ball toward the baseline if the defense is changing positions every few seconds.

The fourth concept for the passer is to look for a target hand. Do not pass the ball inside unless you see a target hand. The passer is often under intense pressure, so he needs some help and a target to aim for. When the post player knows that he won't get the ball until he gives a target, you can bet he will give you a target hand consistently.

The fifth concept is that the feeder should fake his pass before he throws it. This is one of the biggest errors in trying to feed the pivot. The passer does not fake his pass and so often it is deflected by his own defender. The passer should make a short, hard, violent fake to freeze his man for a split second and then pass the ball down to the pivot in another way.

Here are four types of passes a feeder can use: 1. Fake high and throw a bounce pass low; 2. Fake low and throw a two-handed jump pass high; 3. Fake low and throw a pass right by the defender's ear — the defender will not be ready for this type of pass; 4. Fake low and then reverse pivot and throw a bounce pass or chest pass on the other side of your defender. In this type of pass, you want to use your body as a weapon, to keep the ball away from your defender. You are also going to use one of your legs to "lock out" your own defender, so you can get a clear path to throw the ball inside.

The sixth major point for the passer is to give a second look into the low post. You can do this by taking the ball to the baseline and looking to pass it inside. If you can't pass the ball down low, you keep your dribble alive and reverse pivot and start to go back toward the foul line area. You then take one dribble back out toward the foul line and then pivot around back toward the baseline and look to throw a baseline bounce pass. By doing this move, both the defender on the dribbler and the defender in the low post will relax and you can often get the ball into the pivot area.

The final point in feeding the post is to not stand in the same place after you feed the pivot. Most of the time the defense on the post passer will attack the low post man and double him up after the ball is passed in there. The passer should cut the opposite way his defender turns his head to attack the low post man. If the defender turns toward the baseline side to attack the post, you as the passer should cut toward the foul line area. If the defender turns toward the foul line side to attack the low post, the passer should cut toward the baseline. If the defender on you stays with you and does not double up on the low post, you should cut to an open area, but don't stand still. The passer should look to receive the ball back from the low post man if the defender on you doubles up the low post. You should be set to shoot a jump shot or fake the jumper and drive to the hoop as your defender runs back to guard you.

An important note that I have found over the years is that I firmly believe that the bounce pass is the best type of pass to feed the low post man. I feel this way because the defender in the low post area does not like to bend down low because it really hurts and puts a strain on his hamstring muscles. The bigger a player is, the more difficult and uncomfortable it is to bend down low. The offensive player will bend down low because he is anticipating getting the ball and scoring two points. But, the defender in the low post will very rarely have the motivation to get down real low to deflect a pass into the pivot area. He will concede the pass inside and look to block the shot.

Getting the ball inside is only half the battle. You big men must spend hours and hours on your low post moves and fakes once you get the ball down close to the basket. If the perimeter players are going to work their butts off to get you the ball, you need to be able to score and draw fouls, or the effort used to get you the ball will not be as worthwhile.

I know that you have been taught some tremendous back-to-the-basket moves in your stations, but briefly I want to discuss how we try to develop our big men. We begin by spending a lot of time working with our big men individually with no defense. I suggest that you learn only a couple of moves initially, but practice them from both the left and right low post areas. The first moves that you should perfect are the drop step moves, to the middle and to the baseline. When you drop step, take the ball to the rim — do *not* fade away when you shoot.

The second step after you have mastered a few basic moves going to the basket without defense is to play one-on-one with your back to the basket in the low post area. The offense can take up to two dribbles, understanding that the less dribbles taken the better. Next, you should play two-on-two with someone trying to feed you the ball down low. The post defender can play you any way he wants, you will have to adjust to the defense using the ideas and concepts that we have already discussed. The passer's defender must double down and attack the ball. With this type of two-on-two game you are working on posting up, getting position and fighting for position, catching the ball and reacting when you are double-teamed. You can shoot it right away when you get the pass or you can kick it back out and then just play basic two-on-two freelance.

Next, when you have mastered when to shoot and when to pass the ball back outside, you can move on to playing three-on-three. Start by having a high post, a wing and a low post. The defenders on the wing and on the high post must attack the low post when the ball goes inside. The low post man can shoot or kick it back out and then freelance three-on-three.

★ ★ ★ ★ ★

I have shared a lot of ideas and concepts with you today, and I would like to leave you with a quick story. There was a young man named David Moss who was a big-time recruit, a high school Mc-Donald's All-American. The kid decided to go to the University of Tennessee on a full scholarship. After his freshman season he was named the Freshman of the Year in the SEC and was named second team All-SEC. Now you guys know that the SEC is no chump conference, and to be second team All-SEC as a freshman means that the kid had a big-time career ahead of him. It seemed that he had his future ahead of him and that he was a lock for stardom in the NBA. However, not long after his freshman season he felt a knot in his thigh, and when it didn't go away in about a week he decided to have it looked at by the team doctor. Well, the doctor didn't like what he saw and sent him to another doctor who diagnosed it as being cancer. One month after he was named Freshman of the Year in the SEC, he had his leg amputated due to the cancer. One month after the leg was amputated he died.

I tell you this story because so many times you don't know what you have until it is gone. The young man didn't realize how well off he was during the season until he found out about the cancer, and then he didn't know how well he had it even with one leg until the cancer really set and caused him to die. You don't know what you have until it is gone. So I finish today hoping that you will appreciate what you have right now. The good times here at Five-Star, your health, your friends and family can all be cut short or off at any time. Enjoy your friends and family, take advantage of the opportunities here at camp and at your high school, you never know when these may be gone. Don't wait until it is too late, before you realize what you really have.

Rick Pitino captured the country's imagination when he led Providence to the Final Four of the NCAA tournament in 1987 in what was one of the tournament's ultimate Cinderella stories. He has enjoyed success at every stop of his coaching career, including the New York Knicks of the NBA, and is now working his magic at the University of Kentucky. The Wildcats missed the Final Four by one game in 1992 only because of Christian Laettner's turnaround jumper from the top of the key at the buzzer, and made it in 1993. Chances are, they'll be back again.

★Rick Pitino

I was standing in the Statler Hilton lobby across from Madison Square Garden in New York City one day and some very important things in my life took place. The first six months of my senior year of college I had begun thinking about what I was going to do with my life. My first year as a student, I had a 1.9 grade point average, but from then on I did well. As a player, I had played tons of minutes. As a senior, I thought I would be drafted. Much to my dismay, my name was not announced in ten rounds of the NBA draft.

So, I did the next best thing: I signed a contract to play in Italy. Garf came to me in that lobby across from M.S.G. and asked me why I was wasting my time going to play ball in Italy. He encouraged me to go into coaching. I told him I had no interest in coaching.

Then I saw some cheerleaders in grass skirts from Hawaii and said, "That would be nice," just kidding around. Garf replied that he knew the coach and would introduce me. I'm embarrassed, but we go anyway. I asked the coach of Hawaii how to get into coaching. He mentioned the graduate assistant positions all schools had, but told me about the low salary. I said no way, since I was going to make $18,000 in Italy. They had no openings anyway, but three days before leaving for Italy, I got a call saying Hawaii's graduate assistant was going to law school. So I have 24 hours to decide if I wanted to play or coach. I put the ball down to go to Hawaii and work with guys like Pete Gillen, but it didn't work out. It was, however, a great opportunity to break into the field.

Times have changed since I was in high school. Back then, I would pick up my girl at eight and have her home by 10. My girl was an Irish Catholic girl; what I'm trying to say is, there was very little action going on. So you can imagine the wedding night was something special. I just checked into the hotel after getting married that afternoon and I was carrying my bride across the threshold and I am very excited, to say the least. Then the phone rings. I tell my wife that I can't believe her mom would call us at this time. Anyway, I answer the phone and say, "Hi Mom." A squeaky voice on the other line says, "Hi mom? This is Jim Boeheim, the new head coach at Syracuse."

I extended congratulations, but told him that I was beginning my honeymoon. I also asked him how he found out where I was, and he said Howard Garfinkel told him. Why would he do that to me on my honeymoon, at its most special time? I asked Boeheim if he was married, and he said no. He said he wanted to talk to me about being his assistant. I told him that was great and that I would talk to him when I got back from my honeymoon. He said that he was at the airport and that Garf had told him that I would see him. I told him I had no job at the time, and asked if breakfast would be okay. He said no, that he had to talk to me right then. I told him that it was kind of a bad time. At this point, I was thinking he wasn't married and probably wasn't dating too much either. Later I found out he was.

I told my wife that I was going to speak to the guy for 30 minutes, and would be right back. Jim apologized, but explained that he had to recruit the West Coast and wanted to wrap this up. I asked him what he wanted to wrap up and he replied, "I want you to be my assistant." At the time I had some options, but nothing definite. Jim started with Big Orange this and that and throws out $15,000 a year in salary.

Well, we talked for about an hour, then I called my new bride and told her I would be right up. I then proceeded to call back every half hour. Each time I came back from calling my wife, he offered more money, and so by 9:30 p.m. I was up to $19,500.

So I tell my wife that I have good news and bad news, and that I'd be right up. The good news was that I would be making $19,500, the highest-paid assistant in the country, and that she could get a two bedroom apartment and so on. The bad news was that our honeymoon, five days in San Francisco and five days in Hawaii, would have to wait because I had to go recruit some skinny kid in Cincinnati named Louis Orr.

The bottom line is that I had to risk and sacrifice to have been able to coach in the Big East, coach the Knicks, and coach at Kentucky, but it all came about because of two strange things: being in a hotel lobby talking to someone I didn't know, and getting letters written from Chuck Daly and Hubie Brown; Garf got them to write. I also gave up my honeymoon.

I tell you this about my personal life because you need to know that taking chances and risks in the right way can help you make your dreams come true. When I left Syracuse, we were fourth or fifth in the nation. I told Jim Boeheim I wanted to interview with Boston University, not to actually get the head coaching job but for interviewing experience. He said he didn't think I should even bother, because Boston was a Celtics and Bruins town, the university had tough academics, had had three coaches in five years, had no budget, and so on. He didn't think it was a good job to take. I went anyway to interview for the experience.

Two heavy guys picked me up and we talked for an hour, just small talk without one basketball question. We get something to drink and eat and I'm thinking, Now comes the interview. So I have my recruiting programs and letters all ready. I tell them I'd like to talk about fullcourt basketball. They said, "We don't know anything about basketball, we're football guys, but we want to offer you the job." I asked why and they told me that my coach, Jack Leeman, played football at Boston University and told them that I was the man for the job.

Now I'm thinking I have to get out of this job, because you can't win at Boston University. I say "Let's talk contract." I'm thinking I would go for the big bucks. I said five years, but they said one year with a roll-over. If I won, they would roll it over. If I didn't, they wouldn't. I asked about money and they said $19,000, to which I responded that I made $19,500 as an assistant at Syracuse. And the cost of living was cheaper at Syracuse than in Boston. The recruiting budget at Syracuse was $20,000. The Boston budget was $3,000, plus $1,700 for letterhead stationery and postage. I would have one assistant who would be paid $13,000 a year and who would have to teach a class. They went back to discussing my salary and they said they had $2,000 set back for moving expenses that they would add to my salary and that I could have players help me move.

Now I *know* I have to get out of it. They said, "Rick, we know it's a bad job — you'll probably get fired if you lose, but if what we have heard about you is true, then you're the one who can turn B.U. around."

Now, if I told one of you that you are the player who can turn Kentucky around and inflated your ego, you wouldn't come just for that and turn all others down. But I accepted the job. I'll tell you this honestly. I know that I am no better or worse than any other coach in America. I know it for a fact. Who determines if you win or lose? You do, the players. You may fit into the system and make it go. I'm no better or worse than any other coach, but I know one thing: When you sacrifice and are willing to take risks for the right reasons and have belief in one another, you can get it done. We did turn Boston University around and into a winner.

Time goes by and I'm the assistant with the New York Knicks. I'm sitting with a couple of people watching the Big East tourney. I'm about to interview for the Providence job. Garf tells me I'm a fool — I can't win at Providence. I did it at B.U., but at Providence, you're not playing Vermont, New Hampshire and so on. You're playing George-town, Syracuse, Pittsburgh. Garf says don't take the job.

I watch Providence play St. John's, and lose 90-60. This guy hands me a Providence stat sheet. I say I don't notice anything. The guy says that he'd never seen it before, but no one on the team averaged in double figures. Now I know I'm not taking this job. I am not playing Georgetown with this team.

So I go to see the athletic director to say thank you, but I'm going to stay in pro basketball. He looks me in the eye and says, "Each year, we come to the Big East Tourney and get beat in the first game. We are going to change all that and hire you." I am just about to say that I am staying in pro ball, but for some reason I accepted the job.

Here is my team at Providence. This massive individual knocks on my door while I'm at my desk with the stat sheet in front of me and says his name is Jacek Duda. I knew from the name he wasn't from New York. I said, "Jacek, where are you from?" He answers, "Poland." I look at the stats and he had not played in the first two years. He was overweight and I asked what he was doing there. He told me the story of how he defected, enrolled in high school and everybody started recruiting him. I asked him if he was any good and then took him to the gym. I threw him the ball in the lane and with no defense, he goes two-for-10. He didn't know if he was going to stay at Providence, and we were willing to let him leave. I asked him how much he weighed, and he said 280. Then he said that he would be my starting center if I would let him, because Steve Wright was going to flunk out.

So I started reading him the riot act. I told him he had to lose 50 pounds by September, and it was March. He started to sweat heavily and I asked him if he would like something to drink and he said yes, a vodka and 7-Up. I said, "What?" He told me that everyone drinks vodka in Poland. So I gave him a running program and post moves to do. All of a sudden he starts reaching for the pocket on his shirt. I asked him what was wrong and he said that he had been in my office

for over an hour and that was the longest he'd been without a cig-
arette in a long time. So now I'm thinking how I can take his scholarship.
I told him he had to quit smoking and drinking and lose 50 pounds
by September. He says he is my starting center and leaves. I am
depressed. I had just left Bernard King for Jacek Duda.

There's another knock at the door and I see a normal-looking kid
about 6-foot-7 named Dave Kipfer. I ask him where he's from and he
says Toronto, Canada. He says that he is my starting forward despite
the fact that he had zero for stats. Kidding around, I say, "I have no one
else, right?" He says that I don't. I tell him to go out and gain 10 pounds,
and I also gave him a daily workout.

Now, I have Poland and Canada. At the next knock at the door,
a black kid comes in the house named Ernie "Pop" Lewis. Thank
goodness, a normal-looking kid with a nickname, "Pop" — for his
shooting, I figure. I look at his stats — nothing as a frosh and only two
points per game as a sophomore, but he has a nickname so I'm
getting excited. I tell him how he's going to love our style, push it up
the court, press, total freedom, he's going to love it. I figured he was
a 6-4 shooting guard or small forward.

Then he tells me not to get to excited about his shooting. I answered, "What? Your nickname is Pop." He said that he had two older
brothers and his grandfather had named them "Snap" and "Crackle,"
so he automatically became "Pop." This is a true story. I tell him to go
home and work on his jumper, do the workout, and that I would see
him in the fall.

Now, I am going nuts. I have to play the likes of Georgetown,
Syracuse and Villanova with a defector from Poland, a power forward
from Canada who likes hockey better than basketball and a guy who
has a nickname because of a cereal.

The next knock brings a kid named Ryan Ford, who had a huge
knee brace. I look for his name and it's not on the stat sheet. He said
he was a manager last year, but because of all the injuries he practiced with the team and was better than a lot of them. So, I give him
his workout and tell him I will see him in the fall.

At the last knock on the door, in walks a kid who talked real fast.
He says, "My name is Billy Donovan, and I'd like to transfer." He said he
had heard I'd be bringing in a lot of good players, and because of his
love to play he should transfer. I look at the stats, and he had played
five minutes a game as a frosh and six minutes as a sophomore. He
looked very much like the Pillsbury dough boy, with a pouch in his
stomach that held about 30 pounds. He weighed about 190 pounds
at 5-10 ½. He said he wanted to transfer to Northeastern or Fairfield.

I'm so excited, because this is going to free up a scholarship. So I get on the phone to Northeastern and say, "Hey, I've got a Big East player for you named Billy Donovan." They say no thanks, that he can't play for them. Then I call Fairfield and they say that Billy's not good enough for them. So Billy comes back in, and I told him I didn't call the schools. I told him that he was too valuable. I told him I play four guards and that he signed a letter of intent, and that I wasn't letting him out of his commitment. I told him to lose 30 pounds and work on his jumper. I'd seen some film, and he was a push shooter.

To make a long story short, we won 17 games and went to the quarterfinals of the NIT the next year. Everything was going great. We brought in three kids, Marty Conlon, Abdul Shamsid-Deen and Carlton Screen that year. I thought we would be better the next year, so everything was great. This is true. I called a meeting and drew a circle on the board and cut a part of it and talked about academics and overachieving, what they have to do to go to the NCAA. Then, in the middle of the circle, I wrote "N.O." I give them their packets and am ready to go, then Dave Kipfer asked what the N.O. stood for. I told him that it meant New Orleans, where the Final Four was being held that year and that we were going to the Final Four.

I knew what they were thinking. Providence hadn't been to the NCAA tourney in 10 years; we had been dead-last in the Big East up until last year, and we were going to go to the Final Four? "Sure we are. What's wrong with you guys?" I told them that they put limits on themselves. They let everybody tell them that they're too short, that they can't shoot. They let people limit them, so they became limited. From now on, I told them, we were refusing to believe in that philosophy. We then began to dream about the Final Four.

We had one guy join our team the next year, Delray Brooks, a guy who had been named the No. 1 player in the land when he came out of high school. He hadn't gotten any playing time at Indiana University in a year-and-a-half, though, so he decided to transfer. I think he's a 2-guard, and anyway, he chooses us. He comes in and I tell him that I was excited to have him and that I remember him from Five-Star. He responded that he wasn't like he had been at Five-Star anymore, that he didn't have much confidence and wasn't playing well. I told Delray not to worry about it. I told him to get his head up, that there were no limits, and that he was playing on the team that was going to the Final Four.

I forgot to tell you that Jacek Duda lost 58 pounds. He still couldn't play, but he lost 58 pounds. Dave Kipfer bulked up, "Pop" Lewis started stroking the "J" and now the three-point shot is in and he is filling it up. Ryan Ford still has a knee brace and isn't a good players, but he's a great kid. Billy Donovan is on the cover of the press guide and 30 pounds lighter — now he's Billy "The Kid" Donovan, fastest gun in the East. I got him all dressed up in a cowboy outfit, with spurs, boots, the works. Jacek actually thinks he's a player, and off we go.

That year we beat Villanova by 30 points. We beat St. John's with Mark Jackson for the first time in 10 years. We beat Georgetown on national TV to break into the Top 20 for the first time since entering the Big East.

We were playing Georgetown and I got into an argument with John Thompson at halfcourt. What happened was that one of my players jams his finger and I went out to see how it was, and Thompson starts yelling at me. So I go over and he tells me that my team is the dirtiest bunch of so and so's he's ever seen. Well, I say a few things back and now I can't back down as much as I would've liked to. So there I am standing nose to navel with John Thompson. Fortunately for me, nothing happened. We're down one point, with seven seconds to go and Billy Donovan penetrates and dishes off to "Pop" Lewis in the corner. He hits the "J" to break us into the Top 20.

We are now going strong. We beat St. John's again and head into the Big East tourney. Headlines in the Daily News say that Mark Jackson says this is a double-revenge game, that they need the win to go to the NCAA, we don't, and they were going to put us away. So I bring the guys together and show them the article that says we don't need the game. "Can you believe that they think that you are not going to step over that line ready to play," I ask them. "What an attack on your integrity!" All of a sudden, I remember two years ago sitting with those two gentleman watching Providence get beat 90-60. This time the final score is Providence 91, St. John's 60.

So now we play Georgetown in the second round of the Big East tourney. John Thompson walks out, puts arm around me and says, "Hey, no hard feelings. I was just trying to get my team going. But remember, what comes around goes around." Well they beat us by 38 points. It was never a game. We had gotten our guys pumped up, telling them that we were in the NCAA. We had told them that we were going to New Orleans. It was embarrassing. I had learned a little bit about what comes around.

We still were invited to the NCAA tournament, though, and I'm really excited. For the first time in 10 years the Friars are in the tourney, and we're going to take a ton of fans. Well, 37 people show up for our first-round game against UAB in UAB's home gym. So I tell my team we can't take UAB lightly. They say, "It's their home gym, home cooking and all that." I told them that you don't know that the NCAA tourney is 10 percent physical and 90 percent mental. They'll be overconfident which is a big edge for us. They start to believe. We kill UAB by 29 points.

The next night, Austin Peay beats Illinois in a major upset, which is a break for us. But two nights later we think our dream has ended because we're down 10 with four minutes to play. We're already in the final 32, and I'm leaning down listening to the most obnoxious cheer I've ever heard: "The fly is open, let's go Peay." I'm kneeling down and I see their heads down and I say, "It's OK. You're in the final 32. You're not reaching your dreams, but so what. You can be proud of what you're accomplishing. You tried to press these guys and they went through your press, they took away your three. Don't worry about it, I'm very proud of you.

"I'll tell you what, though, there is only one team I know that can give everything they have for 35 minutes and then have fun the last five minutes. They can cut open their chest and tear out their heart and throw it on the ground and change their whole style of play in a five-minute span. But I tell them to promise me one thing: When you get the lead, you won't sit on it and take them lightly." Well, we got very excited and won the game in overtime.

The next game we play Alabama. They have Derrick McKey, an NBA lottery pick, and Michael Ansley, who played with the Orlando Magic, and Jim Farmer, a first-round draft pick for the Mavericks. They were awesome. We saw them play in the first round and they were unbelievable. So I don't think we have a chance, but I bring the guys together and tell them not to get overconfident, that these guys can play. I said, "I know what your thinking — although I didn't. What do you know about Alabama? Football, right? Bear Bryant? You're saying that these guys are intimidated by the New York guys from the Big East. I know what you're thinking, but you can't get overconfident. Yes, they'll be intimidated, no question."

I'm making up a story that makes no sense to calm them down. So we go out and get on fire. It was never a game and we won by 20. Now we are one game from the Final Four with Jacek Duda, Dave Kipfer, Pop Lewis, Billy Donovan, Delray Brooks, some freshman coming off the bench and Steve Wright, who is getting hot in the tourney.

One game left and who do we play? Georgetown. Now I can't give my team a story. So I huddle them up and say, "You're not lucky tonight. You know who's lucky? I'm lucky. I didn't adjust after we beat Georgetown in the regular season. I screwed up. I fed you to the wolves in the Big East tournament. I didn't change anything. I messed up." I told them I had prayed every night for another crack at Georgetown, and that now we had the chance. I told them we were changing everything. We weren't going to shoot the three. Billy wasn't going to bring it up, Pop was, and we were going inside to Duda, Wright and Conlon. In the back of the room, Duda raises his hand and says, "Bad idea, Coach. I can't score on them."

He was probably right, but we had to go inside because they had no double-down principles. I said, "Jacek, who's the most famous Polish person in the world today?" He said, "The Pope." I then asked him who the second-most famous Polish person was, and he said, "Lech Walesa?"

"You're right," I said. "You know, Jacek, when we play Georgetown tomorrow, every television in Poland will be turned to Jacek Duda. (I didn't know if they had television in Poland or not.) You know what, Jacek? If we go inside for you and you score and we beat Georgetown and go to the Final Four, you know what Jacek? You're never catching the Pope, but you are going after Walesa, Jacek, as the second-most famous Polish person today."

My assistant, Stu Jackson, is looking at me like I'm crazy, talking about Lech Walesa and the Polish Army. But we go inside to Jacek, and on an up-and-under move he scores on a three-point play. Wright scores next time down. Duda scores seven points early in the game. I got him out right away because I didn't want to push my luck. We end up winning by 20 and going to the Final Four.

I tell you the story because, as I told my wife, I was coaching the Bad News Bears. But you know what? Billy Donovan lost 30 pounds and believed in himself and became the most dominating player in college basketball at 5-10 ½ — he couldn't be checked. Pop Lewis was a great one. Jacek Duda is still playing in Europe today. Delray Brooks became one of the best three-point shooters in the country. We had the same drills, same teaching of offensive moves, same everything as everyone else, but again it goes back to making dreams become a reality, having no limits.

What do you want to do? Everybody will tell you the stats about how only a small percentage play. Well, you can play in Europe. People will say you can't at 5-10. So many people will tell you not to go after the NBA, but I say you've got to do it. You have to go after the NBA. The average salary is $900,000, the minimum is $150,000. You have to try to make the effort.

We aren't saying not to study. You want to choose a school. Here's what I believe. I'm not giving you a recruiting talk. I don't care if any of you come to Kentucky because there's enough players for everybody. To make your dreams become a reality, you need to find a school where you can play in a style where you are comfortable. Where do you want to settle down? If you graduate from Kentucky, you can get about any job in the state if you're a basketball player. But is Kentucky where you want to settle down? If you want a job in Baltimore, playing at Kentucky might not help you. Give some thought to where you want to live.

You'd better start throwing away your limits right now. You'd better stop letting people tell you that you are limited. Start dreaming right now. If you let people tell you that you're limited, you aren't making your dreams a reality. When I put New Orleans in the middle of the circle, I didn't know what we could do, but we told Billy he was the best gun in the East. We told Pop that he could be great, Kipfer that he could do it in the low post. I just told them what they could do if they believed, and then helped them organize.

Here's what you have to do to be successful. This is what separates dreamers with limits from people with unlimited potential who make dreams a reality. Set your goals and then structure your life. Set definite schedules on and off the court. For example, say, "I'm going to study an hour-and-a-half every night, seven days a week and then for one hour a day I am going to step over the line and work on my game by myself." Not five-on-five, by yourself. And when you structure your life, you may or may not become a pro player or a lawyer or whatever your dreams are, but you are no longer a dreamer, you now make dreams become a reality.

What I want you to do is to put down a few things when you get home for me. First, write down what you want to do with your year, and then put your head down on your pillow and dream of where you are going. Then organize your dream so you can make your dream become a reality. I'll go home and turn on the TV and I'll see another one of you guys put on an NBA uniform. Then I think that one-tenth of one percent make it to the NBA, be real.

Guys, go after the NBA. If you don't make it, you can live with it, but go after it. Be the greatest student you can be. Make dreams become a reality. Organize your life and you're going to look back and say, "I believed I could do it and I made my dreams become a reality." Don't worry about scores on tests, don't worry about all those reasons why you can't achieve your dreams. I wish all of you the chance to be a risk-taker, to be a dreamer, and to make your dreams become a reality. The attempt to get there is what makes it fun.

Marv Kessler's enthusiasm, humor and knowledge make his lectures unforgettable. He played at Boys High School and North Carolina State, then began his coaching career at Van Buren High School in Queens. He moved on to Adelphi University in 1972, leading a team that had won eight games the previous season to a 17-9 record. His 1977 team, spurred on by the tragic death of star player Marshall Williams, is legendary in the annals of small college basketball. Kessler also has worked as a scout for NBA teams and as a championship coach in Venezuela's top pro league.

★ Marv Kessler

At Five-Star, you are going to be overwhelmed with information. You are going to be given some unbelievable stuff, but there is no way you are going to be able to remember it all because you are playing. So what are you going to do? What you need to do is find a Jewish kid to write all the stuff down for you. Get a piece of paper and write down 10 things that you learned each day. Positive things, like how to set a screen, how to run a backdoor, how to feed the pivot, the things that people are looking for.

Sometimes guys don't have the physical ability that other players do, so those less-talented players need to be more creative. I look at a kid like this guy. What's your name? Delray Brooks. Now there's no way that I can physically play with Brooks, but I can play smarter than him. I might be able to get him to turn his head so that I can get a pass for a layup. Maybe then I can get him worried about me, which prevents him from helping out on my teammates. But to play him one-on-one, he would destroy me.

He was born and the doctor slapped him, and he probably said, "Rebound! Shoot!" The doctor slapped me on my butt and I cried. This guy is a very good player and there are a lot of very good players here. When I turn to look at this guy, you know who I see? I see Jimmy Paxson. When I look at that kid over there, the ugly black kid, you know who I see? Darnell Valentine. When I look at this guy, I see Isiah Thomas. When I look at the big black dude, you know who I see? Moses Malone.

Think about it, I could go on and on with the guys who have been at Five-Star. And then I look to the back of the gym and look at the coaches and I see Hubie Brown. I look over there and I see Rick Pitino. On this side of the gym I see Jimmy Lynam. People talk about all the great players that come out of this camp, but look at all the great coaches.

What I am saying is that we get a lot of great players at Five-Star, so what separates the supers from the others? First of all, they came here to learn from these great coaches. The players who became supers came to camp to get better. The coaches here right now will help you learn and get better if you listen, learn, absorb. They also came to find out if they could get it done. That's what you are here for, to learn and to find out if you can get it done. Can you make your high school team? Can you develop your skills? Can you improve your range as you go along? Can you become more creative on your individual moves? Can you learn how to play defense?

Let me tell you something interesting: you will get worse before you get better. It is true, you will get worse before you get better. A player with talent must get worse before he gets better. You cannot get better at Five-Star, you can only get better when you go back home, because you came here with you and your skills. You must improve with those skills. Do not try to be somebody else. You see some kid take the ball through his legs nice and easy and you try to do it and it may come out your butt. Don't try to do things you are not capable of doing. Play your game and improve your skills within that game.

One of the things you will learn is how to play without the basketball. You are going to learn every little thing that will help you. While you are learning, you are going to get worse, because while you are learning you are starting to think. Instead of trying to go one-on-one every time you get the ball, you will begin to pass the ball, because you will learn that the man who just passed the ball will be freer than anybody else on the court. You see, as soon as a man passes the ball, his defender relaxes. As you learn all this, the college coaches will be looking to see if you are unselfish or if you try to take it one-on-one every time. Perhaps you will start to pick up on the fact that when you don't have the ball you can go set a screen and yell to your teammate to "Use me!" This tells your teammate to take advantage of your screen and not go the other direction. You also will know that when you pass to a teammate who is open in his range that you should yell "Shot!" as the ball is in the air to your teammate, because you will know that the passer is the eyes of the receiver.

I have just returned from speaking to coaches from all over Israel at a clinic. There were 900 kids at the lecture. What I am trying to tell you is that there are kids all over the world going to basketball camps trying to get better. You are about one-tenth of one percent of all the kids going to camp. Somewhere in Indiana there is a camp going on. Somewhere in Chicago there is a camp going on. There is competition for college scholarships. There is competition for high school playing time. There is competition all over.

You are in competition right now at camp. One of the first things that I would do would be to learn all the names of your teammates; that is very important. You also need to know your coach's name. You need to know the names of the coaches that are teaching you in stations so you can call them by name and so that you can thank them by name at the end of the week. How many of you will remember all your teammates names all week? How many of you will make the effort to go over and thank Mr. Garfinkel at the end of the week for putting together such a great camp.

With all the instruction that is going on, you don't have the time to not know your teammates' names. You make a cut and free yourself or you set a screen for your teammate and he doesn't see you, you cannot yell, "Hey, yo, man, hey, ha!" You need, "Joe! Irving!" You've got to know your coach's name and your teammates' names.

You also need to learn how to do things like properly setting a screen. If you are setting a screen, you should have your hands at your sides. You should protect yourself by having your hands over your private area, but keep your elbows out. You don't put your fists together under your chin, that's too obvious and you probably will get called for a foul. So from now on, how are you going to set a screen? Now you know how to do it. Go back to your dorm tonight and write it down.

Did you know that you can set a screen with your butt facing the man you want to screen? Some of you didn't know that you could set a screen facing the wrong direction. When you screen that way, the defender isn't tipped off that the screen is coming. Or you can set a screen in the right direction, and after the screen you step to the ball.

These are the ideas that you need to pick up this week at camp. You need to pick up things like catching the ball with the outside eye and seeing the floor with the inside eye. I also know that when I catch the ball with my outside eye I can also see my defender. See, I want to learn the little things about the game. I want you to learn that you have to get back on defense and get in a position to play defense. I want you to learn that my first rule on defense is to not get beat. Don't get beat, that's my first rule on defense. What's your first rule? Is it to try to steal the ball off the dribbler? I know that for every time that you go for a steal on the ball, you are going to miss it three times. I also know that, for most guys, for every blocked shot you will get three fouls.

So what I want to emphasize is how to play within your abilities and contribute to the team. At the end of the week you should feel like you have given it everything you could possibly have given, and when you get home you should take a few days off and get a girl and go to the beach. You should take some time off; I do not believe in playing 365 days a year. Then you begin to work on all the things you learned here, and you start to piece it together. You have learned that when a guy is quicker than you, you take the ball down, and if the defender comes up close on you, then you go by him. If he goes down with the ball, then you bring the ball up, and as he comes up you go by him to the basket, because it is impossible to go up and back at the same time.

You have to have a desire to play or you will never be a player. I had a player on my team for three years named Shapiro. Shapiro was 6-8 and wore a size 17 shoe. I would say, "Shapiro, you want to go in?" and he would say, "No." I would say, "Shapiro, you are 6-8, don't you want to earn a scholarship?" And he would answer, "Not particularly."

I had him for three years, and we lost three games. You know why? Because he had a role. Some of you may not be a great player, but if you understand your role, you can play. Shapiro's role was, when he would catch the ball inside, to throw it back out.

One day he got brave enough to come to me and say, "Coach, I know you have roles, but I want to know why I am not allowed to shoot." I said, "Shapiro, you are a spastic! Every time the spastic shoots, the super has one less shot. Shapiro, do you know the difference between a spastic and a super? A super is Davey Edwards, he has two malts and three bags of potato chips before the game and scores 35. You have one lousy cheese sandwich and you throw up. That's the difference. Davey breaks his finger against DeWitt Clinton and still gets 28 points, and nobody knew his finger was broken. When you sprained your's, you were out for three weeks. That's the difference. When the ball is passed to the spastic, he dribbles the ball out and sets up play No. 2. When the ball is passed to a super, he takes it to the hole, and when he gets fouled he makes the shot and gets a three- point play. When a spastic shoots he misses and looks at his hands. What I am saying to you is that you may not be a super, but you can play if you know your role and perform in it.

I just get the job at Adelphi, and I have this kid Rosenberg on the team. I just get there and am watching the players play some pick-up games, and I get this tap on my shoulder, and this kid says, "Are you Marvin Kessler?" I say yes. And he says, "I'm Rosenberg." He weighs 230 or 240. I say to him, "What can I do for you?" He says, "I want to join the team. The coach last year didn't know what he was doing, and he cut me. Cut me, cut me, cut me."

"Cut you?" I replied? "Yeah, I went in for one layup and he cut me." I said, "Only one layup?" He says, "Yeah, one layup and then I asked for another chance and I threw a bad pass and he cut me again. He cut me five times in one afternoon. Coach, I want to play!"

I told him that on October 15th he could try out. It was June then, and I told him he needed to lose 30 pounds by October 15th. I figured I had run him off, he wasn't going to lose 30 pounds.

But do you know what, he came to practice 30 pounds lighter. I went up to him and said, "What's your name?" He said, "Rosenberg." I said, "Are you the kid who came up to me in June?" He said, "That was me. How do I look? Good, huh?" I said, "You lost 30 pounds?" He said, "That's right, I'm losing weight because that's what you told me to do, and I want to play, and I can play." So he goes out on the court to try out, and he misses his first layup and I yell, "Cut!" Then he throws his first pass away and I yell "cut" again. He says, "All I hear my whole life is 'cut, cut, cut.' "

Anyway, I go home and I tell my wife the story and she says, "You mean to tell me a kid loses 30 pounds from June to October and gets himself in physical condition better than any kid trying out, and you cut him? What are you, an animal?" I tell her, "Honey, this kid can't play." She says, "I don't care, a kid like that, how could you cut him?"

So I went to the bathroom and thought about it. I sat on that stool for about an hour, and I said to myself, What am I going to do with this kid? I gave him a uniform. I figured with his attitude, I could teach him to play defense. He could foul at the end, he could take charges. And you know what? He ended up being one of my great defensive players in three years. Every time a guy got in foul trouble, I'd say, "Rosenberg!" and he'd be there instantly. He'd go in the game and be in a guy's jock. I mean he was crazy! He wanted to play, he wanted to fill a role.

One game we were losing by six points with a minute to go and we were out of timeouts. I sent him in and told him to act like he lost his lens. He said that he didn't wear contact lenses. I said I didn't give a crap, act like you lost your lens. So he goes in and he plays for a few seconds and says, "Ref I lost my lens." So they are on the floor looking for it like you have seen them do, and then he asks the other players to help him. Yeah, he gets the other team looking for it! They're on their hands and knees while we are going over our last-minute strategy.

He didn't wear contact lenses, but he had an act. Great players have a great act. Lousy players have lousy acts. He was a lousy player with a great act. Finally, he says, "Ref, I found it." And he acts like he is putting it in his eye, and the other team is looking in his eye and they are saying, "Yeah, it's in there." I couldn't believe it!

The next game we play like crap and get beat. I was so mad at the refs and our play that I couldn't go into the lockerroom. Out of the corner of my eye I see Rosenberg coming. He comes up to me and says, "Coach, we really blew it. We worked so hard, and then we come out here and let you down. I'm sorry, Coach."

Well, the next game was against a bad team that I knew we could beat, and I tell Rosenberg, "Rosenberg, you've been doing a great job. Tell ya what, you can start next game." My assistants told me that right after I left, old Rosenberg says, "I told you that shit would work."

It's the same thing with playing basketball: you've got to have an act. When you take a charge, you have to have an act. When the contact is made, you must yell "Oy vey!" as loud as you can and fall on your butt — not your hands, but your ass, as you push off with your feet so that you slide. If you don't have an act it is going to be called a block. If you have an act, it is a charge.

Now, let's review some of the finer points of the game. Never pass the ball to a teammate, instead pass the ball away from your team-mate's defender. If the defender is overplaying your teammate, then you fake the pass to the overplay area which sets up the backdoor for your teammate. If a teammate is open in his range, you yell "Shot!" Communicate to your teammates with single word commands, like "shot, screen, help" and so on. Take your man low to go high, and take your man high to go low. Take your man nowhere when you have a dummy guarding you. A dummy is a defender who can't see the ball. The screener is almost always freer than the man he screened for. Remember these ideas and the other ones that we have talked about. Write these things down when you go back to your dorm.

I want to help you, so I am going to tell you a story that I really don't like to tell, but I think that it can help you. I had a player like this guy over here. He was 6-7; I never thought that I would be able to get him. I heard about a kid in my area of New York who was 6-7 and so I went to watch him play. They ran one offense the whole time. He stood at the foul line and they threw him the ball, and the guards would cut off of him. He never posted up, and I got excited because I thought that maybe nobody would see him because of how he was being used. I thought that I might be able to steal him and then when he got to Adelphi I could teach him the post moves and with his strength and size he could be a stud.

But I wasn't so lucky. The same thing I saw in the kid, the other schools saw, because when the ball went up in the air he would follow the shot and he would dunk it in. I really needed a big kid, so I went to see the kid at his home in Bedford Sty. In his home, there were no lights, only candles and very little heat; they were very poor. I said to the kid, "Marshall, I am a city guy. As you know, I played at Boys High. I was the only white kid on the squad. I was the last man in the layup line because I was the only one who couldn't dunk, and they didn't want me messing up their rhythm. I would get about four layups and a couple of jumpers in before the tipoff.

I said, "Marshall, I know where you are coming from." My high school was three blocks from his home. I told him that if he wanted to go to a school near home, he had a scholarship with me. Well, there were some problems at home with his mother, and to take care of her he wanted to go to a school near his home. So, he chose to come to Adelphi. His freshman year he averaged 11 rebounds and 12 points a game, which was very good. We used him down low, but he was such a nice kid that whenever we threw him the ball down low he threw it back out. His sophomore year, when we threw it in he threw it back out every other time, and his moves started to get better. He was getting to the point where teams were having to front him, even though they didn't want to front him because he was such a good rebounder, and by fronting him they gave him rebounding position.

In his junior year we were playing a game and our record was 8 wins and 5 losses. The game before, he had scored 35 points and grabbed 16 rebounds against a Division I school, St. Francis, and we lost by six, giving us our fifth loss. After the game, even though we lost, I came in the locker room fired up. I went in and told Marshall, "I know we lost, but you have arrived! We are going to have a dynasty with you. With Beckers in the backcourt and with McCray as our point guard we have no weaknesses with you." Against St. Francis he wanted the ball for the first time, it was a beautiful thing to watch. His high before that game was only 20 points. He said to me, "Coach I never felt so good in my life in the pivot." I said, "Forget about it, we are on our way, nobody on our schedule is as good as St. Francis; we are going to be a dynasty."

You could set your watch by this kid — he didn't smoke, he didn't drink, he was at practice at 2:30 every day, never late. Everyday Marshall came to practice ready to work and ready to learn. So, the next game gets underway and we throw the ball into Marshall and he turns and scores. We come down again and he scores. We are now running our offense for him. We were drilling this team, we were up by 16 points. Marshall then gets the rebound and outlets it and starts to follow the break. A jump shot is taken and I watch the shot. It bounces straight up, and I'm thinking, Where's Marshall? I look in the lane and there's no Marshall, then I look to the free throw line where he normally is on the secondary break, but no Marshall. I looked at halfcourt, no Marshall. Then I looked in the lane at the other end where he got the rebound and there was Marshall. He was laying on the ground. He must have run a step or two and collapsed.

We went running onto the court. "Are you all right, Marshall? Are you all right?" Marshall was just looking at us, not saying anything. The referees grabbed me and pulled me away and said that he probably just had a seizure or something. I said, "Yeah, but that ain't Marshall. There's no way, that's not Marshall. He's not right, we need a doctor!" So they call over the P.A. and a nurse comes running out. And she put her ear to Marshall's chest and then all of a sudden she grabbed his face and started to breathe into his mouth. Then she said to me, "Coach, pump his chest." I pumped five times and she would breathe, I'd pump five times and she'd breathe. Five and one. Five and one. Five and one. Then she stopped and looked at me and said, "Coach, this boy is dead."

This boy . . . a super human being who stayed at a local college so he could get home to take care of his parents . . . the guy who stayed home so he could work a part-time job . . . the guy who went with me one day to scout a game. I told him, "Marshall, we'll scout the game and then we will get steaks. I know a great steakhouse."

He said, "No, Coach, I don't want steak, I want McDonald's." I said, "What's wrong with you, Marshall? I'm offering you steak, and you want McDonald's?" He said, "Coach, you know it's out of your pocket. This ain't coming from the school. You get a head coaching job in Division I and then I'll take the steak." How many guys would say some stuff like that? "Come on, Coach, just get me a McDonald's, I'm not that hungry."

Then I look over on the bench at the guy who was crying because he wanted more playing time. You give him minutes in the first half and you take him out and he throws the towel! You ask him why he threw the towel and he says that he is mad, he didn't have enough time to get loose. Or the guy who, when a player fouls out at the end of the game and you go to put him in, he looks at the clock and says, "No, not enough time." Those guys are alive and Marshall's dead.

So the team went back and voted to play the season out, but I voted to quit. How are you going to play? You've got a Puerto Rican at 6-4 and a Jewish guy at 6-5. How are you going to play when Marshall was sixth in the nation in Division II, getting 13 boards a game? Why play when it's Division II and we'll get three people at a game, your mother, my mother, and his mother? What's the use? Let's quit.

They said, "No, we want to play, but we want four things. We want something on our uniforms for Marshall, we want the flag at our school flown at half mass, we want the president to collect money for the family, and we want a minute of silence before each game at home and on the road." Then they had a meeting for two hours after they threw me out. I ask them what they are going to talk about and they say that it is none of my business. I didn't care, I didn't want to play anyway.

I don't know what they talked about, but I saw what they did on the court. We put a guard in for Marshall and really took control of the ball. Every time they made a pass or a cut that led to a basket, or anytime they scored a basket or took a charge, they ran down the court and yelled, "Marshall!" When a guy would make a good pass, instead of saying "good pass" like I hope you guys will do this week, or "good screen" like I hope you will do this week, they said, "Marshall." They would get their hands together and they would shout, "Marshall!" You don't have to be a mathematician, because they won every single game the rest of the season. They won 13 straight games and finished 21-5.

I had nothing to do with it except to put the guard in his place, but it taught me a tremendous lesson: you guys can do a lot of things that you don't think you are capable of doing. Those guys made a dedication to win for Marshall, to play defense for Marshall, to shoot for Marshall, to screen for Marshall, pass selection, shot selection, team defense, all for Marshall. A little team beat four teams they had never beaten before in the history of the school. Everybody was going crazy. The athletic director came in and said the school hadn't received an NCAA bid since 1966, and now, 13 years later, we had received an NCAA bid! We were going to the NCAA! But the players said, "Sir, we have already voted, we do not want to play anymore. We do not want to play anymore." He said, "Are you crazy? You just won 13 straight games and you don't want to go to the NCAA?" They said, "That's right. We already voted, 11-0. We played the season out for Marshall. We did what we had to do and we are finished."

I tell you the truth, I was there. I was ready, baby, for the NCAA, but they said no. You mean to tell me that a team can lose it's second-leading scorer and the sixth-leading rebounder in the country, have him die on the floor, and then go out and win every game and then turn down an NCAA bid? But it happened to a little Division II school in a very populated area. Nobody heard about it and nobody knows about it. It took a player's death to bring a team to life. It taught me how little the X's and O's are when you guys really want to play. They weren't spastics, but they were Division II guys that were 5-9 and 6-3 at the forward, not good enough for Division I, but darn good players. We didn't have one guy that shot out of his range or didn't play defense.

I hope that I have taught you that you can do it if you spend the time, and then when it's all over and you are not ready to do it anymore, when you feel your future is shot, that you will be able to say that you gave it your best shot.

Thank you.

Jerry Wainwright isn't a ``big name'' to the average college basketball fan — yet — but his lectures at Five-Star have always been among the most appreciated by the campers because of his knowledge of the fundamentals of basketball and of life. Wainwright was twice named the Illinois high school Coach of the Year, and he's now an assistant coach at Wake Forest. He's destined to become a successful head coach in college as well.

★Jerry Wainwright

I was the seventh boy in a row in a family of 11 kids. When I was eight years old my father took me aside and told me, "Jerry, out of all the boys we have, you are the worst-looking; you are a little on the ugly side." I said to him, "Dad, do you really believe that?" and he said, "Yeah," so I said, "Hey, you know you are messing with my confidence."

I have a beautiful wife now, but she wouldn't go out with me the first few times I asked her. But I continued asking her out until she finally said yes, and I guess what happened was she said to herself, "Maybe if I go out with this guy he will leave me alone." Now we get along great, but I'll tell you something, a lot of you guys are scared of "No." That's why you have pitiful games — you're insecure, afraid to embarrass yourselves by taking a risk. You come here and you're worried about your image. You've got inhibitions, self-imposed guidelines that stop you from reaching your potential.

If you don't risk some things, you'll never know what you can accomplish. The weakest part of all of us is our minds. Did you ever go to the foul line and say, "Oh boy, why did they foul me?" You lose your poise. As a sophomore in high school I fumbled a punt that lost the state championship. It was the seniors' last chance and they didn't talk to me for the rest of the year. One of them was my brother. I had a good football career after that, but when I go back to my neighborhood and guys say, "Hey Jerry, how you doing?" I know as they walk away they're saying, "That's the jerk who fumbled."

They'll always remember me for that, but there's a guy none of you probably ever heard of, Bill Golis, who was my coach at Morton Junior

College in Cicero, Illinois. I'll remember him until I die, which is something he doesn't even know. He taught me poise and confidence. He showed me that a person is as good as what he perceives himself to be and that whatever happens, whether it's good news or bad news, tomorrow it's old news. That's why I'm here. There have been so many people that have helped me along the way, like Coach Golis, that I feel an obligation to give whatever I can back to kids.

One of the most important things you can do for your game is to get stronger. Every one of you can improve not only your game, but also yourself by becoming stronger. I had a high school job in an affluent school district once and there used to be fistfights before every practice to see who would be shirts and who would be skins. That's one of the gravy things about being in good shape. It helps your self-image. You look good. It is also good for injury prevention, making your muscles stronger around the joints, and it can also enhance your skills, making your legs stronger for jumping, rebounding, and finishing plays.

There are a lot of misconceptions about weight training. There is a belief that it can affect a guy's shot in a bad way. Anybody who tells you that just doesn't want to take the time to learn. At Wake Forest our guys work out three times a week, 45 minutes at a time, and afterward they take 50 free throws and 100 jumpers. It doesn't take away from their shot; it actually adds to it. You can very easily develop overall strength without losing flexibility. When I started lifting I used to be into weights and numbers, seeing how quickly I could lift the most weight. I ripped myself up doing it that way. Now I'm into progressions.

There are basically three ways to get stronger. The first is to lift more weight. This may create injuries if your mechanics are not very good. More is not necessarily better. The second way is to lift more times — repetitions. The problem with this idea is that it takes too much time. As basketball players you want to spend as much time on the basketball court as possible. If you have to spend a couple of hours in the weight room every day, then you are sacrificing time that might be spent improving other areas of your game. The third way to get stronger is to cut the rest time down between sets and to put exercises together. This is called supersetting.

For example, if you want to work on the chest you can do a set of bench presses (8-12 reps at approximately 70 percent of max), then do a set of 10 manual resistant push-ups (a partner pushes carefully on your back while you are doing a push-up), then quickly move to dumbbell flys with five-pound weights in each hand, finish up with eight negative dips (start in the up position and control the down part of the dip going from the up position to a position where the elbows are even with the shoulders in 15-30 seconds). If you repeat this superset a couple of times, you will get a tremendous workout.

Obviously, you can apply this superset concept to the different body parts. All you need is to come up with three or four exercises for the major muscle groups. The key is to use weight that you can control, utilize the superset concept of putting exercise together with very little rest time between exercises. Additionally, skipping rope is perhaps the best overall athletic conditioner. It develops agility, hand-foot coordination, rhythm, and balance.

A complete jump rope program, using a weighted rope, improves your physical condition, increases endurance and stamina, and develops upper body and leg strength. When jumping rope, you can feel secure in knowing that what you are doing is safe. Also, you can jump rope in just about any place. For about $5, you can get a jump rope and improve yourself without anyone's help.

Physical strength is one of the most important attributes of a basketball player and probably the easiest thing to improve; however, it is perhaps the most painful and potentially the most embarrassing. In order to gain the outer strength needed for your basketball improvement, you must have inner strength. Outer strength is developed through consistent hard work. There is really no substitute for pushing yourself through your comfort zone. If your workout does not cause pain due to muscular fatigue, then you will not derive the results that you desire. The hardest thing to conquer is your own human nature. The decision to quit or go on will be a battle that you will face during every workout through your entire life. Your body will tell you to quit, but your mind must make you go on.

If you could take a pill with no side effects that would transform your body into the body that you desire, would you do it? Of course you would. Actually, you have that pill available right now; unfortunately, it is in the form of intense strength training and diet. You can have the body that you have always desired, but it will not come easily.

It is important to understand that all of you are at a crossroads in your life, physically. Starting now, if you gain only three pounds a year, getting out of shape more and more each year, by the age of 30 you will be 45 pounds overweight and on your way to having a heart attack, diabetes, and a serious decrease in the quality of life of your life. The habits you form now will be of great importance to your health and weight in the years to come.

We all have weaknesses to overcome. Our biggest weakness is probably the excuses that we can generate in our own mind. Every one of us, if we try, can come up with hundreds of reasons not to work out today or any day. The winners learn to ignore the excuses and reasons that limit one's self and focus on the positive.

Being positive in a situation, especially a situation of adversity, may determine your ultimate success. Every situation or event in your life can be looked at and dealt with in two ways. Does a good performance make you work harder, or does it cause you to "chill-out" because you did so well and your game is solid? Do you pout?

I agree with the philosophy that it is not how hard you fall that matters, but how high you bounce. The way you deal with an event, positive or negative, is more important than the actual event, to me. When you look at things, do you say, "It is possible, but it is too difficult," or do you say, "It is difficult, but it is possible"? Your attitude will make the situation. Some people wake up and say, "Good morning, God!" while others say, "Good God, morning." Which one are you?

There is absolutely no doubt in my mind that each one of us has the ability to control our own attitudes. Even with a positive attitude, it is sometimes very obvious that life isn't fair. I can pick out the smallest NIT player here in camp and have them stand next to the biggest NBA player and you could see how unfair life can be. You need, however, to set the tone for your life right now. Understand, "the race is not always to the swift, but to those who keep running." Talent doesn't always win, but character does. For those of you who are not high school All-Americans right now, as easy as it can be to become discouraged, you must keep focused on the idea that it is better to be there in the end than in the beginning. The difference between failure and success may simply be one more effort.

So what are you going to do when adversity hits? If you don't reach your potential in basketball, it is going to be tough for you to succeed in life. The basic factors leading to success in hoops are the same factors that bring success in life.

One of the most character-changing events in my life came when I was involved in a wreck driving to Five-Star with several players. I was on a four-lane highway, and a tractor-trailer tried to pass me; as he did he clipped my car. I went through the windshield and broke every bone on the right side of my body, punctured a hole in my heart and lost a lung. A story went out over the wire service that I was dead. I wasn't, but I was in intensive care for 30 days and in the hospital for 52 days. For the first 12 days I didn't say thank you. I was mad at the entire world and everybody in it, until they put me in a room with a guy who had Legionnaires' Disease. The man was worse off than I was.

When we compare ourselves to people, we shouldn't compare ourselves to Michael Jordan, we should compare ourselves to those in wheelchairs or who are sick with cancer. You have been given a tremendous gift — it is up to you to use it. Develop your mind, body, and soul. Regardless of your physical or mental attributes or your color or background, there is one thing that is exactly the same for every-body, and that is the amount of time that you have in a day. Each one of you has 24 hours in a day to use as you wish. None of us knows how many days we have, so we can't afford to waste one minute.

People will try to bring you down and cause you to waste your time utilizing peer pressure. If someone dared you to bend over and allow a car's grill to strike you in the head going 60 miles per hour, would you do it? The answer would obviously be no. Yet a lot of you do things that you don't really want to do, or you do things that you know are bad for you because of peer pressure. Each one of you can avoid getting smashed in the head by a car and you also can avoid getting screwed up by drugs.

This peer pressure causes some of you to play below your potential on the court. Making the simple pass or the easy layup does not impress the fellas hanging around they court. Diving for loose balls doesn't get you the oohs and aahs from the boys, but if you base your decisions on what the fans think and want and not what your coach wants, then you'll soon be one of those sitting in the stands. I know that it is tough to live for yourself and not for your peers.

I'll tell you what, I can walk into any classroom on the first day of school and tell you just by looking at where the people sit who the jerks are. It is simple — the pain-in-the-butts sit in the back row. If you make the decision to sit in the back row with all the jag-offs, then I believe you have a problem with your self- esteem. You see, every one of you sell yourself short. You perform at a level below where you are capable because you don't believe you can succeed at a higher level.

It takes a man to do what you are doing here at Five-Star. Everybody wants to say that American kids are soft nowadays. I don't buy that for a minute. I challenge anybody to make it through a regular Five-Star day. At this camp, nobody gets any breaks — you go through stations, you all play two games a day, you all listen to the lectures, you all endure the heat. Let these people who say you are soft try to do what you have done. Nobody is tougher than you guys. At the end of this week you will know in your heart that you did something significant. You will have taken everything the toughest camp in America could give and you will be able to say you kicked its butt.

Don't let anybody tell you that you can't make it, forget the adversity that you may face. You can achieve what you want to achieve when you believe in yourself and are willing to challenge your human nature to give up. This same attitude of determination must hold true in all areas of your life. You gotta have the desire to excel academically. Kids say school is boring. That's a bunch of bull. That is like saying that you know all that you want to know about everything. You can get smarter every day. Do you understand that over 75 percent of all the books in the library are never checked out? And still kids say they didn't have the opportunity to get 700 on the SAT. If your teacher doesn't want to teach you, then learn on your own — read the text book cover to cover. Go to the administration and tell them to have the teacher teach. If you want to learn and you want to get the G.P.A. and the test score, you can do it if you have the desire to work. Simple things like reading 15 minutes every night will allow you to read somewhere between three and six books a month.

My question to you is, are you really doing your best, on and off the court? Lying to yourself is the only way to deal with not doing your best. When you lie to yourself, life becomes a fantasy without meaning. In reality, you can't be yourself. All you have to do is look in the mirror and that guy staring back at you will tell you what you have really done on that day to improve. You are responsible for your own life. If things don't work out, then you are to blame.

As I finish up, I would like to tell you a true story about one of our players at Wake Forest, Sam Ivy. When Sam was a freshman in high school his mother got cancer and it took her a year to die. He went to see her every single day, while still working 35 hours a week as a janitor. During that time he missed a total of one day of school. Sure he could have made excuses to be absent, but that wasn't what he wanted. Sam isn't an All-American, but he is a very good player in perhaps the best conference in the country. Whether Ivy makes a dunk or misses a dunk, his expression doesn't change. He never gets too high or too low. He does his best on the court, in school, and in the weight room. He was dealt a bad deal, but you never heard him complain.

You see, men, success is a journey, not a destination. Each day is important — too important to waste complaining about the adversity that has been set in your way. There is no end point, it is the trip through time that holds the significance. I challenge you to overcome your weakness. Make yourself stronger physically, intellectually, spiritually, and emotionally.

Bob Knight was associated with Five-Star before he or the camp was a big deal. Now he's probably the country's best-known college basketball coach, and one of the game's legendary figures. He has won three national championships at Indiana University (1976, '81 and '87), an Olympic gold medal (1984), a Pan American gold medal (1979) and an NIT title (1979). He has won more than 600 games overall, and is a member of the Hall of Fame. He's still a big part of Five-Star, just as he was when he was a dark-haired young coach at West Point.

★ Bob Knight

Out of over 20,000 players that have come through Five-Star, less than 200 have made it to the NBA. Of 240,000 high school players, only about 3,000 actually play Division I basketball.

Think about that for a minute. That means a couple of you in here will have a chance to play Division I and pro basketball. A lot of you will have the chance to play Division I basketball and there will be some of you who should have the chance to play NBA basketball who won't get there because you'll succumb to something: laziness, drugs, lack of attention. All of a sudden you'll be 30 years old and you'll wonder what happened to you.

Some of you, if we brought you back 10 years from now, it would be just that: "What the heck happened to me? If I were only 18 again. If I could only start this thing again." And there'll be some of you who don't make it as college players for exactly the same reason, and you *should* make it. You've got the world by the butt right now at 17 or 18. You haven't been out on your own. You haven't had to go out and compete with other people just like you guys, so you're the kingpin in your town, your community, your district, your state, anything.

Hey, the woods are full of those guys, boys, and I want to talk to you a little bit about what separates you from other guys just like you all over the country. Why will some of you go on and get a chance to play college or even pro basketball and some of you, with the same ability, not have that chance?

One thing that we take for granted in this country is education. I had a kid working for me from Columbia, South America. Less than 20 percent of the kids there will be able to get a high school education. Think about that. Take advantage of what you've got academically, boys.

I don't think basketball is a game of shots and great plays. There are great plays made in games, but you win because you play the game well. You don't win because you block shots or dunk shots or hit three-point plays, you win because you understand how to play and that involves anticipating what's happening in the game.

I want you to keep this in mind. Playing this game, the mental is to the physical as four is to one, boys, and that's what the heck is gonna separate you as you go along. A kid who doesn't throw the ball away and a kid who doesn't take bad shots is a pretty good player. Given average skills and average athletic ability, he knows what he can do with it. You can learn to play basketball and it goes way beyond the physical skills. Don't worry about what kind of a shooter you are, what size you are, how quick you are. You know you can't teach yourself to grow or to be a heck of a lot stronger or quicker, but you can teach yourself to be a lot better basketball player.

You can have a concept of how to play the game. Very few that play the game have it. I'll use two words for you: look and see. Everybody looks, but not everyone sees. There are players who look and don't see a thing, and there's a heck of a difference, boys.

There are only so many things that can happen in this game. It's an easy game to figure out while you're playing. I can anticipate and then recognize the situation and react to it. Most true basketball players are reactors, but guys like Magic Johnson anticipate. He's the best player in the world at bringing the ball up the floor. If Magic needs to dribble four times, he does. If he only needs to dribble it twice, that's what he does because when he gets it he knows where everybody is. Larry Bird is the best passer I've ever seen without the dribble. He catches it and gets rid of it because when he catches it he already knows where people are. That's not because he has any better vision than anybody else, it's because he uses it. Your eyes are the best thing you have to use in this game. The rules apply to everyone.

Michael Jordan is the best athlete I've ever seen play basketball. In my mind there's nobody else close. There are a lot of athletes as good as Michael, but none of them think like he does. When we had Michael on the Olympic team, if he wasn't playing particularly well I'd

go over and take him by the arm and I'd squeeze his arm a little bit, and I'd say, "Michael, you're too good to play like this," and Michael would just nod his head and say, "You're right," and that's all you had to tell him.

Some guys who are outstanding athletes can't understand what a bad shot is; they think any shot they get is a good one. If you don't understand shot selection, you're going to have a hard time playing at some point in your career. That's why out of thousands only a few have played in the NBA. We're talking about something here that is going to be very difficult to attain, no matter what.

What I'm interested in you having is a chance to play college basketball, and then you just see what happens. To be able to play that way, you've got to be able to put the game together in your mind in a way that you're getting the most out of what it is that you have.

Offensive basketball, boys, is playing without the ball. If you come down and change your position every time down the court, if you make a move as soon as you see the defensive man, if you're gonna play with the ball ... the woods is full of guys like that.

Watching the games here in camp I get the feeling sometimes we ought to build an island for you guards, put all of you on an island over here and play with the forwards and the centers because you guards do more to screw up basketball than the referees do. It isn't even close.

The thing you gotta understand is that you were the guy who set the tempo for everything. How many of you in a halfcourt situation brought the ball down and took a shot? Think about that. Why? I dribble because I want the other four guys involved. If you bring it down you have to get rid of it and you can get it back and shoot it or get it back and penetrate, but I don't want four guys standing while the guard is dribbling. Give it up.

You guards would be amazed at what all happens to you when everybody on your team knows that you're gonna first of all give the ball up and that you're gonna take the good shot after you get the ball back. Think a little bit, guards. You want guys to help you a little bit, to pick up a guy that's loose on defense or somebody rebounding for you? It all starts with you.

How many of you think about the players on your team, who the best shooters are, and you work like heck to set those people up? Or how many of you come down and just make a pass because you've exhausted every move known to man and haven't yet gotten a shot? How many forwards think the guards dribble too much. How many of you get open and you don't get the ball? You've got centers and forwards who are working like heck to get open. They've got to rebound. They're playing the physical part of basketball and a guard has got to help those guys.

Defense can be played by anybody. The problem with this game is everybody thinks about scoring a bucket. When I played guard for Ohio State I was playing once in a game at Madison Square Garden against St. John's. I remember making a driving shot and getting fouled before the shot. I made the basket but is was disallowed. I remember going to the free throw line with a one-and-one thinking about how the bucket had been taken away. I happened to make the one-and-ones, but I didn't think that was nearly as good as making a bucket and that's how we think as players. But the free throw did a heck of a lot more. It got somebody a little closer to foul trouble. It gave us a break and gave us two points. If you understand how to play basketball, you understand that. As a guard, you don't have to dribble down and shoot it. Come down. Get it inside. Make a move. Get it back.

If I'm playing defense and the ball is on the other side of the floor, I know he's not gonna hurt me over here where I am. Chances are you're gonna do one of two things: You're gonna try to move toward the ball or you're gonna wait until the ball comes back to you. I wanna think about where the ball is and I wanna think about trying to stop the ball. Now if my man comes to the ball, then I can get involved with my man, but what can I do playing defense away from the ball? I can be in position to help stop the ball. I can anticipate the drive to the bucket, and then somebody else has to help out where I was.

One year there were nine guards taken in the first round of the NBA draft and only one, Isiah Thomas, was an outstanding physical player. The rest of them were smart, good basketball players and that's where you'll all be separated eventually.

You have to think the game through. You pick up a guy at midcourt, you channel him to his left because he doesn't go to the left very well, or the right. You don't let him penetrate. You're after him all the time. Forwards, be hard to guard on offense. You're playing down inside, you've got to really work hard to get open. You've got to play off the defensive man on offense. If he goes high, you go low. If he turns one way, you go the other way. Too many guys just stand around and wait for the ball to come to them. That's the primary thought most people have on offense, either the ball just comes to me or I go at the ball. The idea on offense is to move to get open and then the ball has to find you. Average athletes can be very difficult to guard because they move extremely well. They are constantly on the move. They are in and out, up and down, and that's the type that's going to be a good player, boys.

Forwards, on defense, make it tough for the first pass to be made. You're down, you're alert, and then you're getting back down the floor on offense. A kid who gets down the floor on defense stops the break just by busting his butt to get here and probably stops two buckets. By running the court on offense, he's gonna pick up two buckets a game and get fouled and that's another two points and now that's the kind of basketball player who can play.

Playing in the post, if the guy is guarding you high, take him a little higher. Keep him there. Get a position, get the ball down low going to the baseline. Don't just stand there and let somebody bring the ball to you. Think a little bit. Don't just go out there and play, boys. Try to come out here and think a play ahead of what you're doing.

It all starts with understanding yourself. Learn your strengths and weaknesses and play away from your weaknesses and toward your strengths. Some of you are not very good perimeter shooters. Some of you don't drive with the ball really well. Don't drive. Give it up and play without it. Some of you are overmatched with quickness on defense. Instead of playing somebody quicker and letting him get past you, play position and learn to give him a little room.

It's a very simple thing, just paying attention to the abilities you've got. Work hard when you're working. How many of you, when you work out, *really* work hard? I could take you right now and work you out and you might say, "I've never worked like that before."

And how many of you, when you work out, work hard on your shooting? You should all have your hands up on that one. And when you shoot a basketball, how many of you say to yourself, "All right, I've got the court set up into six shot areas?" That's about what there are, boys: two at the top of the key, two at the side of the key, and two at the baseline, and then you've got a seventh which is a driving or posting area.

You don't just go out and shoot and dribble a basketball and think that's gonna help you any. You've got to have an organized approach to what you're doing, and when you're working out by yourself you have to demand something of yourself. How many of you, when you're working on handling the basketball, work on handling it in such a way that nobody can take it away from you? How many of you have ever worked hard at dribbling two basketballs at the same time? Why don't all of you take two basketballs in the driveway and work until you can control both of them? If you can handle a basketball under pressure and not lose it, you become a tremendous asset to my team. That's how you learn to play, to develop the physical part of the game, which is secondary in importance to the mental.

We live in the best country in the world. We live in a country that allows us to make choices. We have choices in everything we do. With the choices that we have I don't feel sorry for Len Bias, not in the slightest. He had his own mind and his own body to take care of and just wasn't smart enough to do it. Those of you who have been popping pills and smoking dope are doing the same thing Len Bias did. Those are serious bad shots you're taking, boys, serious judgements that you're using with your body and mind.

Len Bias was better than anybody in here. I've seen you all play and not one of you can touch Len Bias. The only college player I've seen in the past few years as good as Bias was Michael Jordan, and I'm not sure if he was as good as Bias was in college, and Bias is dead. He's not sick and he's not hurt, the son-of-a-gun is dead. He isn't ever gonna play again and you know why he's dead? He's dead because he just wasn't strong enough to take care of himself. Somewhere along the way he wanted to be one of the boys. He wanted to be cool. Well, he was so cool that he's cold right now, colder than heck. That's how cool he was.

You boys will be in all kinds of situations where there are temptations and all kinds of opportunities to do something detrimental to yourself, and when it comes right down to it there's only one person who can take care of you and that's you, yourself. Your buddy doesn't really give a care about you, particularly if he's popping pills or smoking dope. You know what he wants? He wants you right down where he is because he can't handle the fact that you're tougher than he is.

I'll give you a phrase to use the next time somebody offers you some dope: "Stick it up your ass." If he asks you a second time, tell him you know where to stick it and you'll be glad to show him.

Take care of yourselves, boys. Get the most out of what you have. You will see, as you move along in life, the direct correlation of your life on the basketball court with your life off of it. If you learn to play hard and play smart as a player you will have a heck of a chance to be successful off the court. Eliminate your bad plays and your chance for reaching your potential greatly increases.

Jim Lynam has come full circle in his basketball career. He was a starting guard for St. Joseph's College in Philadelphia in the early 1960's, a time when only the elite college teams made the field. He began his coaching career as an assistant under Jack Ramsay at St. Joseph's, then became the head coach at Fairfield and St. Joseph's. Lynam went on to become head coach of the Los Angeles Clippers and Philadelphia 76ers in the NBA, leading the 76ers to the division title in 1990. He is now the 76ers' General Manager. This speech was delivered while he was coaching the 76ers.

★ Jim Lynam

Let me say this initially. I don't do many of these lectures anymore. I don't come here as a basketball expert, I come here because, not so long ago, I was here learning and building much of my basketball reputation. I learned a lot of basketball here from the other great coaches, and I learned a lot watching great players play here — I watched guys like Moses Malone play on these same courts.

I've always been one that believes that you need to always keep your eyes and your ears open because you never know what you might learn. I learned a lot sitting around talking and watching basketball here at Five-Star. Driving up here with my son, I felt a lot of strong feelings. It was 1967 when I first started coming to camp; that's a lot of time, a lot of miles, and a lot of players since my first day with Garf. I am not going to blow in here like some expert and tell you this is what you have to do if you are going to have a chance at making it. No, what I am going to tell you and show you, I swear, is what I do in my gym with the 76ers and Barkley. I don't talk nonsense.

Let me start by saying that it is amazing how stupid we are sometimes. I put myself at the front of that class of stupidity. Please, don't do something dumb. You make a mistake that is so small and you can blow it all. I mean blow it all!

I've got a brother — I'm the oldest of 11 — who made a small mistake. About two weeks ago he almost went tap city. He's not even a crazy guy. He was driving home and fell asleep at the wheel of his car and bumped a tree, bumped a guard rail, bumped a car and bumped his head through the window. Yeah, small mistake. You must be constantly aware of the possible results of your actions. Please, think before you do something stupid.

I'm going to start with a game; the championship game (in 1991). Who was playing? This isn't a quiz or anything, I just want to refresh your memory. Chicago Bulls vs. L.A. Lakers, right? Bulls won, typical locker room scene, everybody hugging.

I want to point something out. First, Bob Costas is freaking out because he can't find Michael Jordan. Costas is the best, but he's going nuts because there's no Michael. Finally the camera finds Jordan. What was Jordan doing? He was holding the trophy, right? No, he was *hugging* the trophy. He was hugging the trophy! What else was he doing? You know, he was crying. Were they fake tears? No, they were the real thing.

Do I know Jordan? Yes, but only casually, I'm not going to lie to you. I know him from working with Nike and through Charles Barkley. I'm going to tell you something. There is not a guy here that wanted anything more than Michael Jordan wanted to hug that trophy. You could be playing cards with him and at some point he would bring up how Detroit put him out for three straight years.

I am going to tell you something, something you don't understand. Do you know how much easier it is to get something if you really, really want it? It is similar to what happens when a teacher asks you what grade you want to get in class. What do you all write down? Yeah, you all write down an "A." It is the same thing when I ask you if you want to be a player. You all say yes! You all want to be a player and you all want an "A" in class. However, when the test comes and you get a 42 percent, then we find out how much you really wanted an "A."

If you want to see how much a guy wants to win, then watch Jordan. Chicago won the first two games in our series with the Bulls in the playoffs, and we are coming home to play them in Philly. My player Hersey Hawkins has to go against Jordan. Hawkins is a great player and one of the all-time great people, but he has to go up against Jordan, and that is a tough thing. We decided to go right at Jordan, show him we mean business.

The first play I say we are going to send Michael a message. But you need to know what you are dealing with in Jordan, because he is so competitive. You know what he does on the offensive end? He is a joke with the ball. Jordan gets the ball and it's like, "Hey Hawk, what's happenin? Relax Hawk." And Jordan just looks at him and Hawkins is like "Aaaahh crap, what's he going to do now?!" Then it is like Jordan is saying, "I'm going to take you right, then *boomp*, give you a little shake, then *boomp*, I'm going to jump, and how's the weather down there, a little cool?" Then *boom*, a jumper.

Here's what Jordan does. He is playing defense against Hawkins while Johnny Dawkins is playing the point. Hawkins comes off baseline screens very well. Jordan, however, acts like he gets hung up on the screen. Now, Dawkins is dying to get Hawk, his running mate and buddy, the ball to shoot an open jumper. But here comes Jordan with his tongue hanging down to his shorts, just as the ball leaves Dawkins' fingertips. Michael jumps into the passing lane, licking his chops, saying like, "Yeah, thanks Johnny."

See, this guy never lets up on you. So we are back at home, down 2-0 in games and I set up this genius play to start the game. See, Jordan never lets Hawk touch the ball the first few plays, so I clear the side out and I tell Hawk to take him out to about the three-point line and back-cut to the goal, and if we can get you the ball, even on a lob, and you score the first basket on Jordan the first play — wow, old ladies in the Spectrum will be high-fivin'!

Hawk is going for the ball and cuts backdoor, but I know Jordan will not let him get the backdoor. I tell Hawk he has a good chance of getting the ball on the wing. Yeah, right. I know this guy, he will never let his man handle the ball on the first play of the game. So Charles Barkley is to come across the lane and back pick Jordan, then just in case somehow Jordan gets through, Armond Gilliam is there to set another screen. And then the last guy to be waiting to ring Jordan's bell: Rick Mahorn.

So, Hawk runs backdoor off of Barkley, then off Gilliam, then off Mahorn. I expect Hawkins to be able to catch the ball, finger the seams, eye the goal and shoot his wide open jumper, but guess what? The ball is in the air to Hawkins and as Hawk catches the ball it is like, "Hi Hawk, it's me, Mike!"

Are you kidding me? This is a 50-point scorer if he wants to be. And I see you guys, a little brush screen along the baseline and you are like, "Help, switch!" Come on, guys. Look around you. What you have here are basically normal human beings. But are you going to call Michael Jordan a normal human being? Come on guys, this guy is like he just came down from the planet Pluton. Normal? How about the play in the championship when Jordan goes down the lane as Perkins is about to help and he jumps, brings the ball back and dunks on about three people? Yeah, that's normal.

I have actually seen guys trying to practice the dunk Michael does when he takes off about 20 feet from the goal and dunks it in a horizontal position. It reminds me of the days when Dr. J did all his one-hand stuff and people actually tried to do what he did, only they had normal-sized hands.

One thing you *can* be is tough and competitive. The individual that I think is the toughest no-nonsense player is a guy by the name of Michael Cooper, who used to play for the Lakers. I'll tell you a story. It was late in the season and the L.A. Clippers were playing the Lakers and the Clippers were something like 27 wins and 57 losses while the Lakers were nine games up in first place. It wasn't supposed to be a competitive game. Norm Nixon was running the baseline using screens from 7-2, 290-pound James Donaldson. Finally, they call an offensive foul on Donaldson for setting an illegal screen on Cooper who was guarding Nixon. Well, Cooper squares off with Donaldson, Donaldson has never been in a fight in his life and he is trying to keep Cooper off of him. Finally, Donaldson just palms Cooper's head while Cooper is still swinging. It was a funny scene. After it is all broken up they had to throw Cooper out of the game because Cooper wouldn't calm down; he wants to kill Donaldson.

Six months later we're playing in a pre-season exhibition game and Norm Nixon catches a skip pass about foul line extended to the three-point line. Donaldson is on the lane just below the foul line. Just as Nixon is about to catch the ball, here comes Michael Cooper sprinting from across the court full speed. As Donaldson begins to turn, he sees Cooper coming; his eyes got as big as silver dollars. Cooper proceeded to blast Donaldson so hard that they're still looking for parts of him in the gym.

Michael Cooper is a competitor. It's like the definition of a thoroughbred. The great horses are called thoroughbreds. You bring out two thoroughbreds before a race and they will get after each other like nobody's business. The horse doesn't say, "Put some more hay in my bag and I'll compete." No, if he's a thoroughbred, you don't have to tell him to compete. Being competitive is something that you've got to have if you're going to be great.

I've asked Garf to get six guys out here to demonstrate some things for me. I am going to ask them to do something I don't like to do and that is to let their man catch the first pass on the wing. I don't ever tell my players to let their man catch the ball. See, in the real games with real competition, you don't *let* anybody get open or catch the ball. One of the problems here is that some of you have great talent, but are not challenged by thoroughbred competition.

I would like for you three offensive players to pass the ball to the wing and try to score. So that we can get into this quickly, let the pass go to the wing, then "D" up hard. Notice I didn't tell them how to score. When we run play No. 1, we don't say Hawkins gets the shot and on play No. 1-B Barkley gets the shot. A competitor utilizes the situations in the proper manner.

Also, in our offense we tell Hawkins to play off the baseline. Does that mean he must come out this way? No, I let him play the game, because Hawkins is a good player. A lot of the guys who try to make the 76ers come into my gym, get open in the corner and get the ball and have Charles Barkley posting up on the block and they can't get him the ball. The guy in the corner can do all that bull crap, dribble through his legs and so on, but he can't throw the ball to Barkley. Feeding the post is a basic part of basketball. I don't care about rules, just get the ball to Charles in the post.

OK, we have three of the top players in camp out here trying to pass the ball to the wing and score. I didn't give them any rules, except pass to the wing and score. Here is what I saw. One of the top guards in camp was unable to throw the ball into the post. One of the top forwards in camp couldn't catch the ball in traffic. These are two of the most basic things in hoops. I promise you, if Hawkins throws the ball to Barkley, Barkley will catch it if he can get his finger tips on it. He is a competitor; he'll catch the ball.

Let me ask you a question. What are the two things that excite the crowd the most? I believe they are, No. 1, the dunk and No. 2, the blocked shot. Who's the best shot-blocker in the game? Manute Bol. He can block shots like you cannot believe. You may not like his game, but he can block shots. You should see what players do to avoid Manute blocking their shots. Now, when you big guys get the ball, one of the first things you do is dribble the ball. After you take a dribble, the only real thing you can do is out-jump 'em. When you limit yourself like that, it is no wonder you get your shot blocked.

Instead of immediately bouncing the ball you can do, in my opinion, the most effective move in basketball: execute the shot fake. Why not catch the ball and pump fake? Guess who catches the ball and shot-fakes better than anyone who has played the game? Without question it is Larry Bird. Larry will shot-fake seven times on one possession.

Have you ever seen Charles Barkley try to guard Bird? Charles loves guarding Bird because he is so competitive, but when Bird sees Charles guarding him he gets this big grin on his face. He loves Charles and he loves playing with Charles' head. The first time Bird comes off a screen Charles wants to not just block his shot, he wants to send it into Row 12. Here comes Bird off a screen. You all know him, he can't run and he can't jump 12 inches high. He catches the ball with Barkley right on his butt. Bird catches it and pump fakes. Charles explodes up somewhere into the rafters of Boston Garden. Meanwhile Bird is going, "What's up, Charles? Come on down here so I can get three." Understand that there is nothing wrong with getting your shot blocked or getting pump-faked; it shows you are competitive.

Here's something I do with my point guards. If you young guys think you can penetrate, here is a good test. Start with the ball at the top of the key. Defense start with your hand or forearm on his chest. Other defenders cannot be in the lane. The only thing I am going to tell the point guard with the ball is to go by the defense and try to score. No foot fakes or anything, just blast by the defense right or left staying in the width of the lane.

Stopping guard penetration on the perimeter isn't an easy thing to do. I want to burst out laughing when people ask why the Lakers let Paxson shoot all those jump shots. Chicago is a very good team; they move the ball around and guess who comes up top and gets the ball? Michael Jordan does, and they empty out the side. And here is poor Magic Johnson guarding Paxson, Byron Scott is up guarding Michael shaking like a leaf wondering if Jordan is going to beat him right or left and hoping he doesn't get hurt on the dunk. What does Michael do? He blasts past Scott right or left down the lane, draws Magic and knows that Paxson is in the corner — you know the rest.

It all happened because of penetration from the top. What if Michael couldn't penetrate, then Magic doesn't have to help and Paxson doesn't get the jumpers. My guy demonstrating this drill did a terrific thing. His defender was up on him too tight and he did exactly what he should have done. He dropped his head and went to the goal. Anytime a man plays you too close, drop your head and go. You will figure out what hand to dribble with; trust your instincts with those decisions. If you have a good dribble move, you only have to use it one time. If you need two dribble moves on a possession, then how good was the first one? I tell my players, get a good dribble move and you will only have to use it once and you will blast past the defender. If you don't need to use a dribble move, then don't.

When I look for a player, I want one that can beat his man; he must be able to penetrate. I gotta have a guy that can beat his man. Now we are going to add the only other thing that can happen at 8 p.m. on game night, and that is to add the help defense. If you are going to help on the penetration, do not allow a layup. I'm not saying hurt the man, but never give up an uncontested layup. The game now is to dump the ball off when the defensive help stops you.

This is the game of basketball; you drop your head and go by the defense. If the help comes and stops you, then you kick the ball out to the open man. That is the game oversimplified. You don't need three foot fakes and all that crap, just go by the defense and make the play.

I have one saying in my office. The 76ers don't have their own building so our office space is limited. My office is the size of a high school junior varsity coach's office. I have no pictures or anything in my office, I only have one saying taped up on my wall. It is: "There is only one problem with being on top of the world, and it is that every 24 hours the world turns upside-down." This saying is so true, especially in basketball. You may have a great game today and then the next game, whether it is a better player guarding you or you just don't make your shots, you play lousy. You may have great talent today, but if you don't work at it and play hard in the games, then your world may be upside down before you know it.

We have seen it happen too many times here at Five-Star. These supers come in here with great reputations, only to get knocked down by some unknown dude working his butt off to make a name for himself. Nobody is safe; you gotta keep working or your world will be turned upside-down before you know what is happening.

I will leave you with one last story that I saw with my own eyes on television. It begins with a video of this little black kid playing a piano at about age five. This kid from Baltimore started messing around on the piano at about age three. In the house was the mother, father, and one brother and after a few weeks or so they noticed that he had some talent, so they got him lessons. It started out being once a week. By the time he was in first grade he was going to his lessons everyday. They couldn't keep him off the piano! The kid was blind since birth; he has never seen the keys, man.

Now, at age 14, he is playing the piano at Carnegie Hall, totally blind! So it isn't about having somebody show you another dribble move, it is about really wanting something. Just like the blind kid from Baltimore playing the piano, if you want something and love something enough, you will pick up the technique. It is the love and the desire that really makes you great.

James Brown knows from experience how important it is to prepare yourself for a career outside of basketball. One of the top players in the country coming out of high school, he put his academic skills to good use by attending Harvard. Although a standout player there, the NBA career he had always dreamed about didn't pan out, forcing him into the "real world" sooner than expected. He's made it as a widely respected basketball analyst for CBS television, however, proving that hard work and preparation bring success off the court as well.

★ James Brown

By learning and paying the price, an individual can realize success. I came out of high school as a high school All-American and decided to attend Harvard University of the Ivy League. What I learned during the course of my college career was that you must work just as hard to stay successful as you do to taste success for the first time.

To stay successful or to achieve success you must be in tune with the fine points of the game of basketball as well as the seemingly basic fundamentals. I know that you can add two points to your scoring average just by getting the ball to the triple threat position immediately upon receiving the ball. A player can add four points a game by becoming a great free throw shooter. If you can make free throws, instead of going six-for-10 at the line, you can go nine-for-10 and also put yourself in a position to have things set up so that you have the ball at the end of the game rather than someone else on your team. In turn, you will be the individual getting the extra foul shots at the end of the game and will have added at least four points to your scoring total. The little things of the game many times turn out to be the big things when the competition increases.

The first phase of my career was very successful. Being one of the top-ranked seniors in America coming out of high school and going on to have a very good college career made the first phase of my career an enjoyable experience. However, this phase created complacency. I thought that my talent would put me in the NBA. I somehow believed that my game was good enough that I didn't have to stay after practice and work on my weaknesses, that I didn't have to continue to improve.

The second phase of my career was not so pleasant. Because I had not worked to stay on top of my competition, I was cut by the Atlanta Hawks. I didn't pay the price to realize success at the next level. Phase two in your life may be going from high school to college. Regardless of where you currently are, you better continue to work or you will be passed by. Staying the best player in your area is just as difficult as becoming the best player in your area.

So, after being cut by the Hawks I was forced to move to phase three — the game of life. In the game of life there are no timeouts and the tests come rapid-fire. I want to share with you some thoughts that may help you, whether you are in your phase one, two, or three. Please don't let an opportunity to succeed slip by you because you were not prepared.

I believe there are some common threads of success. When you are finished playing basketball you all are going to have to get a job. Many times the quality of a man's life is in direct relation to the quality of a man's job. Being in a position to do something that you enjoy and being able to earn a living by it makes life more enjoyable and satisfying. You need to gain the threads of success now that will allow you to become involved in a career of your choice later. These threads of success do not only apply when you finished playing ball, they are important now. The sooner you learn to put them into your life the sooner you will be able to achieve success and remain successful regardless of the endeavor.

First, improve your communication skills. Learn the King's English and be sound when you write and when you speak. How you communicate will play a big role in your being hired for a job. If you cannot express yourself in an effective manner, then it is doubtful that you will get the job that you desire.

When you apply for a job, you almost always have to have a resume that explains what you have done, and if the resume is impressive enough — written well and void of mistakes — you will probably be called in for an interview. At the interview you will need to express yourself in a professional manner that is understood and accepted by all those interviewing you. If you cannot field the questions and respond effectively, you will not get the job.

Whether you like it or not, you need to learn to speak like professional people. The slang and the way a lot of you speak among your friends will not get you the job that you desire. Every one of you can become a better writer and speaker. In nearly all schools and libraries there are a number of books that will help you improve your writing skills. Additionally, learning grammar rules will help you communicate more correctly and make you appealing to an employer. You may think that you do not need to speak and write well because you are so young, but if you do not learn now it will be very difficult later. Improve your writing and speaking now and you will put yourself in a position to be successful later.

Next, developing personal relations skills are important, not only to your high school basketball team, but also to any job that you may have. No matter what direction you go in life you must be able to get along with the individuals around you. If you cannot get along with your teammates, chances are that you and your team will not reach your potential. Teamwork in the business field is just as important as teamwork on the basketball court. In business everybody has a job to do, a role to play, and many times your job depends on working with those around you. You must be a team player if your company is going to be successful. Playing basketball is one of the best things you can do to prepare yourself for the personal relations that are so vital in the corporate world. Learn to get along with everybody on your team and you will be making a big step toward making it big in the work world.

The third thread of success is to constantly search for intelligence. You do not have to be a mental giant to obtain intelligence and knowledge. I hope everyone of you can read. So much can be learned in such a short time if you make the effort to read on a daily basis and read positive things. Also, each of you has the ability to listen to the people around you, especially your teachers. I suggest that you make the effort to ask questions during class and also after class. You will be amazed how much you can learn by asking a few extra questions every day and then concentrating on the answers. Intelligence is out there for anybody to grasp — you must be willing to make the effort. If you gain knowledge you become a person that is worth more and with that worth comes enjoyment. Intelligence is a very important ingredient to success.

The fourth thread I would like to share with you is in the area of reliability. Make a vow to never be late, ever. Your punctuality will make a statement about your character. A man that is always on time has prowess. If you can be counted on to always be on time, you will gain respect. Doing what is required goes along with being on time. If you do every homework assignment, I really believe that you will learn more and you will become more disciplined. You know that being a disciplined individual will lead to success. I encourage you to be a person that everybody can count on. If you say you are going to be someplace, then be there. If you tell a friend that you will be at his home at 9 a.m., then you should be there at 9 a.m.

The last thread of success deals with your dress and attire. How you dress makes a statement about who you are. When I first graduated from college I had a job interview for a very good job that payed extremely well. Being the big-time basketball player that I was, I thought I would go to the interview as I wanted to dress. I was dressed in the fashion of that time. I had my afro puffed up about a foot high, I had my shirt unbuttoned down my chest, I was wearing a big, thick necklace, and I had on some extra high platform shoes. I went into this very professional corporation attempting to get a job dressed the way I was and I was eliminated before the first word was out of my mouth. It did not matter how intelligent I was, how well I spoke, or how well I could relate to people, I was not going to be hired due to my appearance.

You might not like that, but that is how the world works. In a job you must be willing to conform to the company's standards — if I wasn't even willing to dress appropriately, then I probably would not conform to the company's expectations and would in turn be eliminated as a candidate. Your attire does make a statement about yourself. As you look around at the successful people in America notice how they dress and how neat they are. It doesn't cost much money to look professional. You never know who you might meet and how they might be able to help — make sure your first impression is a positive one. Many times your first impression is the lasting impression.

If you arrive on time, look sharp, give a firm handshake, look the individual in the eye, communicate well, have the ability to get along with others, and possess intelligence, then I believe you have made a super step toward being successful in phase three, the game of life.

Terry Tyler was rock-solid throughout his 11-year career in the National Basketball Association. He rarely missed a game in his seven seasons with the Detroit Pistons, three seasons with the Sacramento Kings and one season with the Dallas Mavericks. The first player drafted by the Pistons in 1978, he averaged in double figures in five of his seasons in Detroit, and ranks among the Pistons' all-time leaders in games played, rebounds and steals, and is the team's all-time leader in blocked shots. The insight and experience of this Five-Star alum have made him a welcome coach and lecturer at camp.

★ Terry Tyler

Let me start by saying that you are only going to be 16 years old one time. If you don't take advantage of the opportunities in front of you right now, you are going to regret it down the road. Get the most out of your coaches, teachers and friends — you never know when you won't be able to enjoy them or learn from them anymore.

Don't take them or this opportunity at Five-Star for granted. When I started playing basketball, the thought of playing pro basketball seemed easy. Because I was blessed with some talent, many things came easy for me, but as you move up in this game you are going to find that the road gets more and more difficult with each year. In the NBA you play three games in five nights, and those games are not against individuals that take it easy on you. Let me tell you, there is nothing easy about the game of basketball when you are checking Karl Malone in the post.

You have to have mental and physical toughness if you are going to get to and last at the NBA level. You see, after banging heads with Michael Jordan on Monday, you have to be ready for a bout with Karl Malone on Wednesday, and then you travel across the country and try to cover Larry Bird for 40 minutes on Thursday, and then you get to check Dominique Wilkins on Friday. If you think this pro game is easy, I've got news for you, it isn't. If you want a chance to play in the league, you had better learn to be competitive right now. Competitiveness is vital to being a pro. It doesn't matter how much physical talent you have, if you aren't willing to compete you will get wiped out in the pros.

Success to me cannot have a dollar figure attached to it. Playing pro basketball is a dream that I have been fortunate to achieve, but just because I've played several years in the NBA doesn't mean I am successful. I have to work every day to keep that dream alive, because the fans and the G.M.s don't remember what you did last year if you aren't getting it done this year.

"Terry Tyler, you're not good enough anymore; you just been put on waivers." I worked hard to keep from hearing those words any sooner than necessary. I hope that you are working and listening now to keep your coach, regardless of the level, from telling you a similar statement. It is one thing to play ball, but it's a totally different thing to get better each day. How hard do you work? Are you working on the right things? I hope that you are not wasting your time. It is better to spend 40 minutes at full speed than spending three hours working at a level that you will never play at in a game. Make your practice time efficient.

Additionally, don't be afraid to get embarrassed. I was on a Michael Jordan highlight getting dunked on. I was on CNN more than 20 times, getting dunked on in front of a national audience each time the highlight was shown. However, if you never risk getting dunked on and run away from dangerous plays to save your pride, you probably won't ever get dunked on the way I did, but at the same time you probably won't ever make a great play, either. Don't be afraid of being embarrassed, it is the only way to improve. Seek out the best competition. When you play pick-up games, guard the best player on the court. Take a chance; that's how you improve.

We all have people we look up to, people we idolize. My basketball idol was David Thompson. I really respected how he played. I loved how he would hang in the air and how he would create positive plays out of situations that looked like nothing. You might someday become somebody's idol, like David Thompson was for me. You might be a young kid in your hometown's idol right now.

But just because you have achieved some success, don't think that success will protect you from the evils of society. Terry Furlow was a player that many people idolized for his basketball prowess. He had a serious game. He averaged 30 points a game and was on his way to being a super pro basketball player, but somehow he thought he was too good or too successful to be affected negatively by drugs. One night Terry Furlow was out partying and tried to drive home all messed up on drugs. In his expensive Mercedes Benz he ran off the road and into a telephone poll. He snapped his neck in two places and died. All the work he put in on his game was instantly gone.

Everybody says it will never happen to me. I imagine Terry Furlow thought it would never happen to him either, but it did.

My mother went into a coma after I went to college and eventually died. I would give all the success I have achieved to get her back. Every trophy, every dollar I have earned, would be given away immediately to have her back. I can't get her back, gentlemen. I had and have to deal with that adversity. My mother said to get my degree, and I have that degree now. What I think my mother was telling me was to use basketball as a means to and end, not an end in itself.

I have also found out that there is more to life than playing ball, and life will continue after basketball is over. I am now married and have three sons. When you have a family of your own, it becomes clear that basketball is only a game. The game can be very rewarding, but it is a game. Use it, don't let it use you; there are a lot of things more important. My career is almost over; yours is just beginning. When one door in your life closes another door will open, but you must make it happen. Make it happen *now*. Don't wait, you never know when it will be too late. In this game of basketball and in life, remember that you are only as good as your last jump shot. You have got to constantly improve.

I'll leave you with three points of advice:

1. Get your education. It will last a lot longer than your jumper.

2. Stay away from drugs. Drugs don't care who you are or what you've achieved.

3. Thank the person who was responsible for your coming to camp. Love your mom and dad, they are the best friends that you have and they are not replaceable.

Evan Pickman isn't a household name around the United States, but he's a legend at Five-Star for his coaching and lecturing. Pickman used to scout the East Coast for the Los Angeles Clippers of the NBA, and is a tenured health and physical education professor at the College of Staten Island. He is a master instructor of the finer points of the game, such as defensive stance and setting picks — hey, they don't call him Pick-man for nothing.

★Evan Pickman

For many years, I coached and taught with some degree of success, but it wasn't until I started working the Five-Star Camp that I have finally developed a philosophy of life. Basketball, and more specifically Five-Star, stands for and teaches much more than a game. My lecture today is about how to be a better student of the game of basketball and life. After 24 years of teaching, I finally know my philosophy of life and that is that I cannot allow myself, my family, or my students to settle for mediocrity.

The system in America has allowed us to settle for mediocrity. Parents allow their kids to get "C's" when they are capable of "B's." People just get by. Don't allow yourself to just do the minimum — focus on the subject in school and don't accept a 70 percent in the class because it is easier than doing what is necessary to get a 90 percent. What you do in the classroom will carry over into basketball.

We have become a country that accepts mediocrity. Just look at the movie reviews; notice how many two-star movies there are. A two-star movie is a dog, but we cannot produce five-star movies anymore, so we settle for a poor movie. Restaurants are rated on a four-star scale, but nobody expects to eat at a four-star restaurant.

My job as a coach and educator is to not only teach the subject matter but also to teach you how to do more. How to *not* settle for being average. What kind of son are you? What kind of brother are you? Do you ever do anything extra for your family?

I believe there are four things that you need to do on a daily basis to go beyond what the majority of America is doing. These are the minimums that you must demand of yourself.

1. *Show up and be on time.* One-third of all New York students drop out of school after they turn 14 years old. The attendance rate for students and workers throughout the United States is terrible and is getting worse every year. People don't go to work and class because it is too hard. They are tired or a little sick, and rather than fighting through the adversity, they stay home. I believe that if you make a commitment, you must honor it. By your being at camp, you are ahead of thousands of people your age. Do you go to class? If you blow off class, then you are on you way to mediocrity.

The same thing goes with being on time. Your punctuality is another way of showing if you settle for mediocrity. If it doesn't bother you to be late, I would bet that soon it won't bother you to not show up. The first minimum is to show up and be on time.

2. *Listen.* A lot of you hear, but you do not listen, and there is a big difference between the two. "Focus" is an important term in basketball. You can really learn basketball by simply listening. Listening requires an individual to concentrate on the speaker, and like showing up on time, it requires fighting through distractions and adversity.

3. *Look and see.* Some people can only learn by doing and messing up. If you can learn from other people's mistakes, you are going to be ahead of the competition. When a concept is demonstrated, don't daydream or let your mind wander, focus and learn from the mistakes of others. You will be amazed how much you can learn if you let other people be your first trial-and-error.

4. *Practice real.* Do your homework real. Study without the radio or television on — focus. If you practice real Monday through Thursday, when the test on Friday comes you will be ready to do more than average. The same is true on the basketball court. If you work out at game speed every day, when the real game arrives you will be ready to perform at a level above mediocrity.

When I teach these four skills, I have made a valuable contribution. Athletics is about doing more than average. Don't be a two-star or three-star player and person, be a five-star player and person. If you do not do these four minimums, you will remain mediocre.

You will become a better player if you understand why. Understanding why you do something enables you to do it more effectively, because you understand the concept behind the skill. Understand that the six-through-twelve members of every NBA team are just as talented as the top five, with the exception of the superstars. The difference lies in that the top five understand NBA defense, and they understand how to use screens. If you want to be a player, you had better watch and listen today because it will be noticeable if you don't. Coaches expect you to know things at the higher levels, and it shows up in the games if you don't. There are a lot of great athletes who will never play in college or the pros because they can't think and they can't remember things they've been told.

Why do we set picks? The answer is we want the defense to think. That's when they start making mistakes. The easiest job in basketball is guarding the man with the ball. It doesn't take any brains. All you need is heart. All you need to do is say to yourself, "I don't care what this guy does, there's no way he's beating me." If you get beat five straight times, maybe you should think about taking up tennis.

The second easiest job is denying your man the basketball. It takes no mind at all. It's all attitude, so what we want to do is make the defense think, force them to make mental errors. That's how we get good shots. To do that, we have to be in control. To set a pick, the most important thing is timing. Time the screen so the man using it can read it and time his movements accordingly.

On the screen off the ball, the screener should first find the defensive man and get a good stance. Do it like you mean it. Look at how I'm doing it, look at my legs, gentlemen. This is the stance you want. Stand firm with your knees bent. Keep your hands close to your body or it's a foul. If you are coming from behind, give the guy one step. If you are on the side, peripherally, you can go right up next to him.

The hard part is using the screen. A lot of guys are too anxious. They don't have enough patience to let the screen develop and then they whine to the coach that the screens don't work. It's because they're moving too soon. The first thing you do when you see the screen coming is move your defender away from it. Fake away from the screen and make it a real fake. No disco moves. No dancing out on the court, you can save the dance moves for when you go home and are working on the ladies. Make your fake "Memorex." In other words, make it real. You must run your man into the screen. Brush your teammate on the way past him.

The screener must be alert. If the defenders switch, he should execute the spin move and pin the defender by pivoting, getting low and wide and then calling for the ball with the defender on his back. You can't relax in this game.

If it is a screen on the ball, the man with the ball must make a decision after he has taken the defense away from the screen. If the screen is on the left, the man with the ball must go right so that he sets the defender up and so that he creates a good screening angle. Again, this fake must be real. As the dribbler comes off the screener, going by shoulder-to-shoulder, he makes the decision to go to the goal, shoot the jumper, hit the roller going to the basket, hit the roller stepping back, or hit the roller fading to the open area.

This decision must be done at exactly the right time. What the dribbler does is created by what the defense does. For example, if the defenders switch, then the roll man has a mismatch and the dribbler should pass to him rolling to the goal. If the defenders double the ball, the screener should find the open area that creates a good passing angle. If the defender guarding the screener makes a strong hedge move, then the screener might pick and pop for the jumper.

Now we have got the defense thinking and making mistakes on the screens on and off the ball. What do they do? Do both defenders follow the guy coming off the screen? These are the things you must read. Don't make a weak pass, especially you big guys. Maybe in high school you're never out on top, but there are a lot of 6-foot-8 guys playing guard in the NBA. It is a shame to make the proper read and then blow the play with a soft pass.

The key to the whole thing is to communicate, gentlemen, and I don't mean with words. This is a new level. Everybody can talk and hear, but the Division I way, the big-time way, is communication with your eyes. Look. See the whole floor.

My last question to you is what do you do when there's no practice scheduled, no homework given, or no coach watching? What you do on your own when nobody is making you work will determine if you are going to be mediocre or not. Patrick Ewing works on his game and strength three hours a day almost every day. Michael Jordan comes back after every summer with a new move. Magic Johnson came out of Michigan State without an outside jumper and as a very average free throw shooter, but he developed into an effective jump shooter and one of the league's best free throw shooters. Ewing, Jordan, and Johnson refuse to settle for being average; they work on their games when practice isn't scheduled and when the coach isn't watching.

Are you going to be like them, or are you going settle for mediocrity?

Brendan Malone got his coaching start at Power Memorial High School in New York City, where he coached for six seasons. He ``graduated'' to college coaching at Fordham in 1976, moved on to Yale a year later, then worked six seasons as an assistant at Syracuse. He became the head coach at Rhode Island in 1984, then joined Hubie Brown's staff with the New York Knicks in 1986. He was an assistant to Chuck Daly on the Detroit Pistons' championship teams in 1989 and '90, and has assisted Ron Rothstein and Don Chaney in Detroit the past two seasons.

★ Brendan Malone

You must believe in yourself before you can ever be a truly good player. Many people will tell you that you are not good enough, but if you have a strong belief in who you are and how hard you are willing to work, nothing they can say will keep you from your goal.

Tom Garrick didn't believe he was a Division II player while he was being recruited by Bryant College. Garrick hustled his way to Division I and Rhode Island University, and then into the NBA as a second-round draft pick of the Clippers. Hersey Hawkins had to beg to get a scholarship at Bradley. Dan Majerle was a virtual unknown player when he was at Central Michigan University, but he made a name for himself at the Portsmouth Camp after his senior year. Majerle went on to make the Olympic team and then became a first-round draft pick in the NBA. Scottie Pippen was a Division II player and made the Chicago Bulls and is an NBA star. Mark Jackson was rated the third-best point guard coming out of his class in New York City. Jackson never lost his confidence and became the 18th pick in the NBA draft for the Knicks and was Rookie of the Year.

Mental toughness is the most important ingredient in the NBA. With the number of games that are played each year (82 in the regular season), if a player doesn't have the ability to bounce back after a negative game or experience, then he will be cut or put on waivers before he can get through a 10-day contract. The thing that makes the supers all-stars is their ability to perform night in and night out, regardless of injuries, distractions, and adversity.

Before we draft a player, we hire a private eye to do an in-depth personal report on the individuals we are considering. In doing this report, the detective will interview just about everybody that had significant dealings with the player. Many times the player's friends will come out and say negative things about the individual, so as to tell the truth to the detective. Nowadays you must be responsible for your actions. You cannot get away with things today without it being found out later. If you pay attention to the draft previews and then the actual draft you will see at least one or two players drop 15 to 20 spots in the draft. You can bet many times this is due to the information compiled in the personal report.

Also, you have probably seen a big-time high school player never make it in college. This happens because some individuals cannot handle success. They get the idea that they don't need to work anymore. They let early success spoil them. Don't be spoiled by your early success. And at the same time don't let early failure spoil you; Pippen and Majerle didn't. If you are not one of those high school All-Americans, don't be discouraged; you can pass them up if you have heart and dreams.

Heart and mental toughness are nearly the same thing. Rebounding is often a good indicator of your heart and toughness. Rebounding is mainly a desire to get position and then attacking the basketball. When offensive rebounding, go to a spot opposite the side the shot is getting ready to be taken from. As you get to this spot under the basket, work your way out using your lower body to gain the territory. Players like Moses Malone, Charles Oakley, and Paul Silas have made a lot of money using this basic technique.

When the rebound is taken off the defensive glass, the rebounder should try to grab the ball with two hands and execute a half turn in the air away from the rim. As this turn is being made, he should look for his man to throw the outlet. The quicker the outlet can be made, the better the fast break and the more easy baskets for his team.

Specifically, the fast break is not a situation similar to a track meet, but is a situation of control. The break begins with a sharp outlet to the point guard. The point guard should get up the court as far as possible and position himself near the sideline to improve the outlet pass angle. He should have his butt facing the sideline so as to be able to see the pass and the potential defenders trying to intercept the pass or get the charge. If the point guard cannot pass the ball ahead, he should get the ball to the middle of the court as soon as possible. The individuals running the court should run wide and must see the ball at all times. Running close to the sideline, the player should run to the hash mark and then cut to the block. When they hit the block they should either go through the lane and out to the opposite wing or jam and pop out to the wing for a spot-up three pointer.

The point guard should know who is on the wing. Is the person a king or a queen? In other words, can the player on the wing catch the ball, can he put it on the floor, can he finish? The point guard must make this read and react accordingly.

If it is a two-on-one situation for the offense, the offense should go wide and try to bring the defensive player out of the lane. If the defender is not on the offensive man with the ball's path, he should take the ball to the rim and try to dunk it or lay it in. If the defender is on the man in the ball's path, he should make a bounce pass with the hand closest to his teammate, while being under control so he avoids the charge. If the offensive man without the ball sees the defender pick up the man with the ball, he should move to the dots or broken line area in the middle of the lane with his hands up, knees flexed and ready to receive the pass and explode to the goal.

The three-on-two situation and two-on-one situation become opportunities that you begin to successfully complete if you practice them with the proper knowledge of how to attack them.

Practice, with intensity and imagination, becomes a player's best friend. Everybody can come up with excuses why they can't work on their game, but the great ones get it done, regardless of the obstacles.

Rafael Addison, a former great player at Syracuse, had to get up at 5:30 a.m. to have a court to work on his game. The opportunity to work out later in the day by himself was not available, so he made the commitment to get up early and walk some distance to a goal that was bent at the base and had a bent rusty rim with barely a net on it. He was there every morning working on his jump shot. A lot of you won't shoot on a goal unless it has a net and is ten feet high. Addison didn't let a pitiful basket, a long walk, and an early wake-up keep him from improving himself. You can make yourself a good player by dedication to your dreams. Through work and sweat you improve.

Knowing something like "a ball fake is a shot not taken or a pass not thrown" is a thing than can make you better. Knowing that if you're feeding the post and the defense is playing you halfway, you take a dribble toward the defensive man and either make the pass or shoot a jumper can help your game. Or knowing that if you are three-quartering the offensive man in the post and you feel him leaning on you that you can release contact, slip around and get the steal when the pass is released, this can help you become a better player. However, nothing can take the place of hours on the court. Forget about the obstacles, get out and make yourself better though practice.

Don't let heat or a lack of confidence stop you. Greatness begins with a dream. A few years ago Jim Valvano gave a lecture here at Five-Star where he spoke of his dream of winning an NCAA championship. He actually got out a ladder and scissors and cut down the net in front of the entire camp. The very next year he won the national championship. He realized his dream with work and mental toughness. Everybody will tell you why you can't make it. But everybody told Muggsy Bogues, and Mark Jackson, and Chris Mullin, and Dan Majerle the same thing. You determine your destiny, your critics do not. Dream your dream and work to make it happen.

Most people know Chuck Daly as the stylish coach who won consecutive world championships with the Detroit Pistons and a gold medal with the Dream Team in the 1992 Olympic Games. But Daly has earned the spoils of his success. He started out as a high school coach, and has climbed the ladder as an assistant at Duke, the head coach at Boston College and the University of Pennsylvania, an assistant with the Philadelphia 76ers, and then the head coach with Cleveland, Detroit and New Jersey in the NBA. This lecture was given after the Pistons won their second title, in 1990.

★ Chuck Daly

I am not going to give you a sermon today. Yes, we have won back-to-back NBA championships, and I did say *we*. The year before our first title we were in a position to win it. Some people say we should have won three in a row, but it doesn't work like that. If we had won that one, we might not have won the other two.

I am going to talk on a variety of subjects today, some of which will be basketball. First, I have a few questions, but I don't want an answer — I just want you to think about them. The questions are, first, why are you here, and second, what do you hope to take away from this camp? I know what this camp stands for. I watched its progress for all of its years. First, you're playing against the best personnel in any camp. You are probably getting the best instruction that you can possibly receive in a camp situation. The most important thing is, what are you going to do with it?

I watched last night's program — I thought it was excellent, but I also know that many of you thought it was a joke and won't use the great ideas. Those that didn't listen do not think they need to improve their game. A lot of you think you already have all the answers on and off the court. I understand that. But sooner or later you are going to find out that isn't true.

I've been coaching this game for 35 years at just about every level. The hardest part of my job is not coaching in the finals or coaching in the playoffs or regular season, it comes on October 12th when we leave to begin our exhibition season. This is the most difficult time because we will bring in 18 or 19 players, and only 12 can make the team. I'll have to tell seven of them that they aren't on the team. This is tough because like a lot of you, they have dreamed of playing ball.

Let me ask you a question: How many of you think you can play Division I basketball? Now lets go a step further. How many of you think you can play in the NBA? I asked Garf the question last night. He has a real good idea of how many of you can play at the Division I level and how many might be able to play in the NBA in time. He told me that perhaps 10 of you will make it. That is what you should shoot for, but what you need to prepare for is what you are going to do if you don't make it to the NBA.

I want to talk about the financial aspect of basketball. Before I took the Pistons' job, I had just come off a TV job in Philly. The year before I had been fired at Cleveland after only 93 days on the job; I had taken over a team that had won 37 games the year before.

An interesting thing happened in Detroit. My daughter was going to go to college at Penn State and wanted a Pistons shirt, a simple T-shirt with "Pistons" on the front. I went to a shop in the Detroit airport and they had the Detroit Red Wings, Lions and Tigers, but nothing with the Pistons on it. But with only 37 wins that was understandable. So I thought I'd go to a department store or a sporting goods store — surprisingly, there were no Pistons shirts in these stores, either. So I thought I'd go to the organization to get one. They had no shirts, even in the promotion department. They didn't believe they could sell a shirt with their logo on it.

Now, let me take you to six years later. They sold 30 million dollars worth of Detroit Pistons merchandise. Thirty million. We were playing in the Silverdome, a football stadium. We had as many as 63,000 people at a game because of good marketing, but they weren't making the kind of money they wanted. So the owner and two other guys decided to build a new building. Last year, we moved into the building with 22,000 seats. The seats on the floor are $100-plus, like most arenas. We have 180 boxes because our owner had a very unusual foresight. Most arenas have maybe 30. We had $11 million dollars in the till because the boxes in the 17th row are $120,000 each. We had 11 million in the till before we ever sold one of the 22,000 seats.

Next, let me tell you about salaries. You all say you want to play in the NBA and make the big salaries, which you should. Walter Berry, who was a first-round draft choice out of St. John's, went to play in Europe. They signed him for 38 million dollars, a guy who never played one game in the NBA. And John "Hot Rod" Williams got an offer for somewhere around $25 million for seven years as a sixth man.

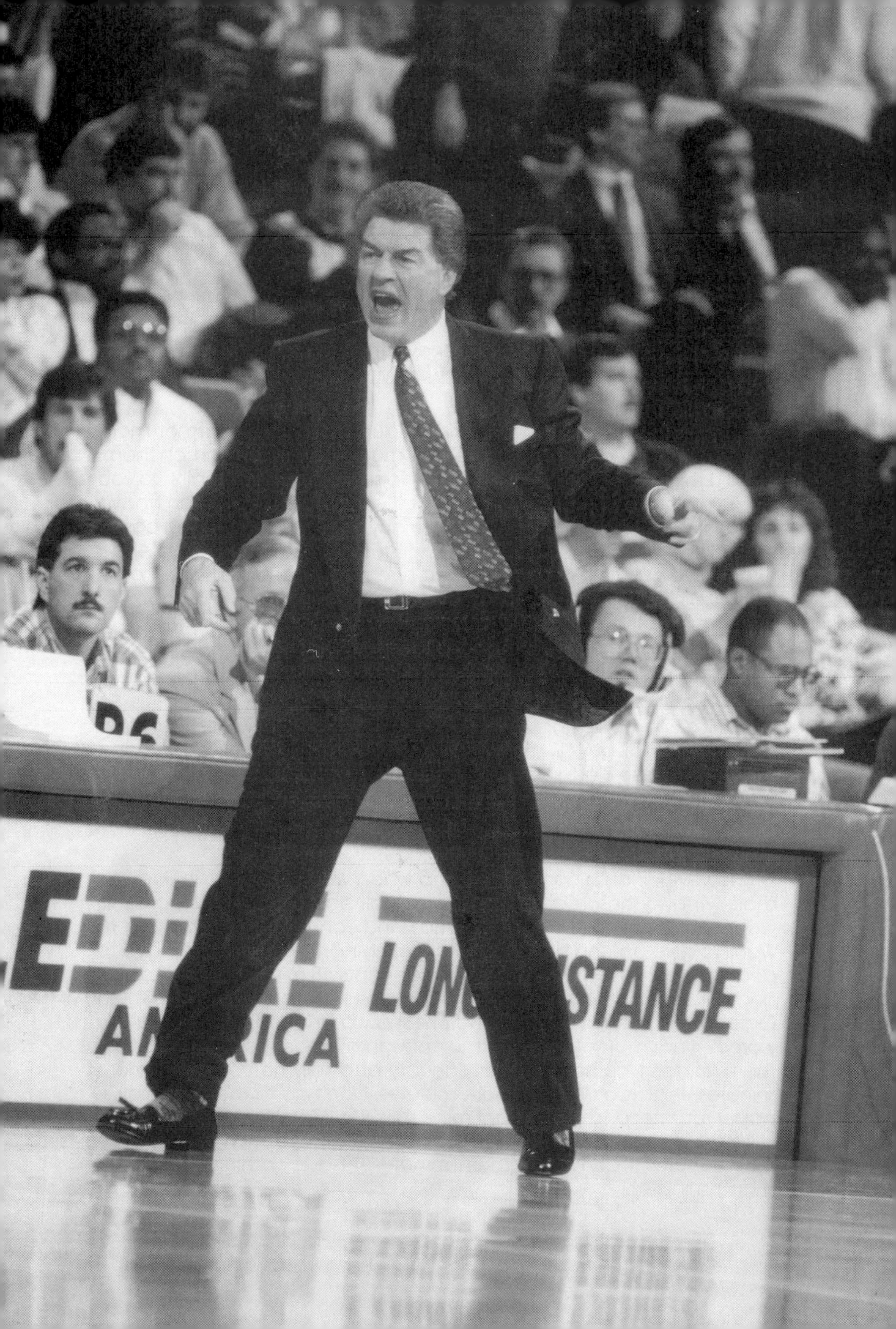

That's the financial part of the NBA. That's what some people can look forward to. That is why I asked the question how many of you think you can make it. The next thing I say to you goes back to the first part, that some of you think you are too good to work on your game and someone like me will have to cut you from the roster. I had to cut one of the great players of all time in Spencer Haywood. It was one of the toughest things I had to do. The money is there, the opportunity is there, but some of you may be your own worst enemy in terms of developing your skills as a player.

Again, I watched last night, and I guarantee you that not more than five of you will take those ideas home with you and work on them. Do you think you have enough moves to shoot the basketball? Do you think you are quick enough, jump well enough that you won't have to do all these other things? We had a guy come to our training camp who played at Texas, an interesting player, Lance Blanks. I watched him for five minutes. I never watched him shoot, because I didn't care if he could shoot or not. I have a bunch of guys who can't shoot, like Rodman and Salley.

Now I know that's where you all spend your time. But we have to have guys who do other things. We have to play the screen and roll night in and night out, and I know how difficult that is to execute. So I'm sitting with (assistant coaches) Brendan Malone and Brendan Suhr and we have six guys working out. I tell them to set up the screen and roll, I want to see Blanks on defense. I didn't care about him offensively. So I watch him on defense and I really liked what I saw. I told my assistant that I thought the kid had a chance to make our roster and play in the NBA.

However, Blanks comes to camp when we already have Joe Dumars, Vinny Johnson and Isiah Thomas all signed. Blanks is going to want minutes while Dumars, Thomas and Johnson are not going to want to give up one single minute of playing time. What we have to deal with in the NBA is that every player wants 48 minutes and 48 shots, and they get upset if they don't get their shots and minutes. On October 5th, we have a meeting. We show a film and then I say a few words — not many, they hear me enough all year. The one thing I tell them is, don't come to me in January and tell me you want more minutes, that you deserve more minutes. Don't go to the local newspaper reporter and say, "I want more minutes." Tomorrow morning you will start to determine whether you deserve minutes or not. They earn their minutes, I don't give them minutes. I have nothing to do with giving minutes.

Our responsibility as coaches is to win games at whatever level and to get guys to play together. Coaches need to decide how they are going to do it and how they are going to sell it. A lot of people wouldn't like to play for the Detroit Pistons despite the fact that we've won two world championships and have our own plane, because we average 90-plus points a game. We are a defensive-minded club in everything we do. A lot of people think it is strictly defense, but a lot more of it has to do with the offensive end. We are not going to run up and down the court during the regular season and score 118 to 122 points a game and then change our game in the playoffs. I see that happen at the pro level and also at the collegiate level. You see some of these running type programs at the college level score 140 points, 130 points, and then teams begin to really prepare for you and they take many of those points away from you.

So I made a decision several years ago to play playoff basketball all year long. We know that if we get 30 fast breaks a game during the season, then we will only get 20 in the playoffs because they are going to take things away with intensity. Our guys are no different then you guys. They want to score, and scoring makes the game what it is, but they have also found out that the rewards are much greater for winning than they are for individual stats of any kind.

Two years in a row the media picked a first, second and third all-NBA team. Guess how many of our guys, who won a world championship, were on those teams? None! Last year they picked the teams again and we had one player make the second team and that was Joe Dumars, not Isiah Thomas. Isiah did not make any of those teams, but in the championship series he was named the MVP. He is capable on a given night of doing almost anything. You may have seen him a few years ago score 16 or 17 points in about 90 seconds.

The bottom line is that our guys have decided to go along with our philosophy at the defensive and offensive ends. We don't throw the ball all over the place and we try not to take wild shots; I'd like to say we're perfect, but we're not. I'd also like to take credit for it, but I can't. In this league, you are only a manager of talent. You are not going to win if your people are not willing to do everything necessary to win at both ends and are willing to police themselves.

I'd like to show you a few things regarding basketball. We are known as a good defensive basketball team, a physical club. A lot of people do not like our physical nature. I want to show you some of the things we do that may help you become better using three guys in shirts and three in skins.

First, the guy bringing the ball up the court must be able to get the ball in a position to start the offense. If the guard has to turn his back to get the ball up the court he is in big trouble, because we can do too many things defensively if the point guard turns his back. So as a guard you have to be able to keep the ball in front of you and you must be able to see the floor against pressure defense.

Offensively, I want you to run a simple, basic action that is run at every level of the game. The point guard will bring the ball up and pass it to the forward who must free himself on the wing area below the foul line extended. The center (5) will position himself at the foul line. When the guard hits the wing he should cut off the center who screens at the foul line. The guard must get to the block. After the center screens, he steps back for a pass from the forward (3). When the 3-man passes to the 5-man, he sets a down screen for the one man who uses the screen to pop to the wing looking for the jumper or post feed.

Now here's the defensive instruction: We want the defensive man to really pressure the ball, attempting to make the opponent turn his back and not be able to beat him and go by him. I want the wing to get in a stance and make it very tough for the 3-man to receive a pass. He does this by getting a low stance with the hand straight out in a denial position with a palm facing the ball. The man defending the 5-man must be ready to help on the cutter. After the 1-man makes a pass to the wing (if he can), I don't want you to let him cut to the block — chest him all the way.

One thing we and a lot of other teams do is not to let teams go where they want to go. If you are playing a great player and you let him go where he wants to go, you are in big trouble. If you watch our team play, you'll notice that we get into a lot of fights. Part of the reason for this is that when guys like Larry Bird or Kevin McHale come down the court, they want to go to their spot, catch the ball and score. If we let them catch the ball on their spot, we can't stop them, so we don't let them get there. We will always chest and use the forearm and never let them go where they want to go.

I'm amused when I watch the college game and people run the passing game because the defense lets them cut where they want to go. When people play the passing game, we simply do not let them go where they want to go. If the 1-man comes off the screen hard, his defender must follow him hard off the screen and then get into the passing lane. If the 3-man screens, his defender must step out and forearm the 1-man if he curls. The 3-man's defender must stay behind and follow hard to destroy the timing. The defense must keep playing.

When the ball goes up, you must box out. I tell my team every single game that we can't allow second shots. If you don't allow second shots, you can't possibly lose a game. However, nobody wants to box. Everybody talks about us defensively and how good we are. Understand that Bill Laimbeer is a mediocre defender at best. We are a little above average man-for-man, but we have also found out that the important thing defensively is rebounding. Don't let people go where they want to go. Take them out of their pattern.

Offensively you need some basic concepts. First, don't screen air. If a defender starts to slide over the top of a screen, then move up on him. If this happens, the offensive player must fade. A common term in our league is to take what the defense gives you. College coaches look at our offenses and think it is all so old-fashioned and simple. But try to play with it or against it and you'll see how difficult it can be.

Every coach knows that if you have a player with a lot of athletic ability, you can teach him some things and make him effective on the defensive end. This is probably the best drill I have ever seen or used to teach defense. We used it just about every other day for years and years. It's called the hedge drill. It is a series of screen and rolls. In our offense, we use a screen and roll on most possessions with Isiah or Dumars on top, at the beginning of the offense. But when you play Cleveland you had better be ready for a screen and roll later in their offense, not at the beginning.

The player guarding the point guard must put great pressure on the ball and get over the top of the screen without switching. The player guarding the 4-man must provide total help. The player guarding the center must hedge. Keep your hand on the offensive player, but I want you above the screener and out.

Every aspect of defense is total man-to-man defense, simple things offensively and defensively but done well. If you don't want to work, you cannot be a good defender. "Work at it, work at it" is a term we use over and over every night. Play 48 minutes!

Back a few years ago, we were having some big problems on the team and I called the players together in the middle of the floor inside the jump ball circle. I can tell a lot of things from the middle of the circle. If a guy has two feet in the circle, you know he's involved with the program. The guy that's not sure has one foot in and one foot out. The guy with both feet out is truly mad and not with the program, concerned more with individual stats than team results, which causes the team big problems.

You need to decide where you want to be. What do you want to take out of camp? When I started coming to this camp, all the college coaches were here. Times change. Academics will get harder. Drug problems, I've seen them. Everybody says, "I can handle them." We all know that if everything is equal the guy not doing drugs will be better. What do you want to do academically, and with drugs and alcohol?

Somehow you are going to have to make the decisions on these ideas. You are going to get all kinds of information on these subjects and most of you are going to blow it off. You are also going to have to make the decision as a player. I talked about the financial end of it, what you can do with it and where it can take you. I just happened to appear at a golf outing a few weeks ago with guys like Dean Smith, Dave Gavitt, Larry Brown, Doug Moe, Billy Cunningham, Michael Jordan and Julius Erving. We played 36 holes with 14 guys, then sat around and ate in a very informal setting.

One night I sat with Julius Erving, who I had the great opportunity to coach when I was on the 76er's staff. He's one of those guys who is at another level with respect to his demeanor, style of play and the way he handles people, and we got talking about players in the league. One statement he made stuck with me. He said that when he came into the ABA and NBA, he asked himself how he wanted his story to end.

I think you need to ask yourself that question — how do you want your story to end? Maybe you have the ability to make the NBA, maybe you don't, but you need to decide how you want your story to end. In Julius Erving's case, he's America's best; every time you turn around he is representing basketball in a positive way. Everybody wants him to endorse whatever they are promoting because he knew how he wanted the story to end.

I hope when you leave here today, regardless of what you learned from me, if anything, or what you got from the camp, that you start to decide how you want your story to end. Start doing your own story, and take into consideration your academics, your lifestyle and your basketball career.

Clark Kellogg is living proof of why basketball players, even the super-stars, must prepare themselves for a life after athletics. Kellogg was a high school All-American in Cleveland, the Big Ten's Most Valuable Player at Ohio State, and a standout player for the Indiana Pacers of the NBA. He played three complete seasons, averaging more than 19 points and nine rebounds per game, and brief parts of two others before a knee injury forced him into early retirement. Now, however, he is a rising star in the broadcasting field, providing analysis for the Pacers and for college games on CBS and ESPN. No doubt about it, this man has practiced what he preaches.

★ Clark Kellogg

I can't help but think back to when I was in high school and when I was your age. I am trying to think back to how I would try to learn from a speaker, what I would try to gain. I hope that I can give you something to help you move on as a person and improve as a player.

You see, I am a "has been" now! My basketball career is over, finished, but I have tasted success at every level of the game. I was once a high school All-American at Cleveland St. Joseph's High School, and still hold the single-game scoring record for the state of Ohio's Final Four. I was the MVP of the Big Ten while playing at Ohio State, I was the eighth pick in the NBA draft by the Indiana Pacers and went on to make the All-Rookie team. I was part of the awesome class of 1979 — guys like Isiah Thomas, Sam Bowie, Ralph Sampson, James Worthy, Terry Cummings, Dominique Wilkins, John Paxson, Dale Ellis, and many other great players. Furthermore, I was on the verge of being a truly great professional basketball player when all of a sudden I did something to my knee. The doctors thought with surgery, some time off, and rehab I would be back to normal in a month or two, but when I went back on the court the swelling reappeared and surgery couldn't fix it. My playing career was over. The book of my life was moving to a new chapter, whether I was ready or not.

What I discovered in being part of the class of '79, however, was that it is not enough to just get by. It is vital to get the most out of what God has given you. Only a few players get to the NBA. The levels of basketball are similar to a triangle. The base of the triangle is junior high and high school basketball; the players at this point number in the thousands and thousands. Moving to the next level of the triangle eliminates many players; this level is college basketball, and more specifically Division I. The last level and peak of the triangle is the NBA, where only about 350 individuals make it.

So what weeds the players out from one level to the next? The answer many times lies in a person's attitude. Not working in the classroom eliminates many, as will lack of dedication to working on the fundamentals. Failing to stay away from drugs and alcohol weeds out several more, and sometimes players' personalities keep them from achieving the level they are physically capable of achieving.

Each level — high school, college, and pro — has the same foundation for success and failure. What choices do you make? What kind of attitude do you have? Nowadays everybody wants to be like Mike (Jordan), but who wants to work, sweat, and condition like Mike? Hard work is a vital part of the success or failure foundation.

To have the foundation for success, you must dare to be different for the right reasons. You can destroy what you have worked years to obtain so quickly just by being in the wrong place at the wrong time. What governs your actions and choices? What do you do and what choices do you make when your coaches and parents are not around? Do "your boys" govern your decisions, or do you try to please God and your parents? The answers to these questions probably will determine how far this game will take you.

We can all make excuses for not accomplishing our goals or not reaching our potential. Excuses are easy to come up with. Anybody can feel sorry for themselves or blame others for their own shortcomings, but to build a foundation for success in basketball and in life we must learn to make positive choices that call for positive action.

You have got to give something to get something. Nothing is free. The game has become so competitive that you must continually work to gain an edge. Many times that edge will be the difference between making it to the next level of that triangle or failing to reach the next level. What goes in the wash comes out in the rinse. You know what kind of effort you are making. You can fool a lot of people, but don't try to fool yourself. You know what you are putting in.

What would you like others to say about you when you are not around? Do your actions cause others to say positive things about you when you are not around? What are you doing to prepare yourself for life? The same positive characteristics of a good basketball player carry over into life — discipline, sacrifice, hard work. What type of foundation are you laying for your future family? Will you be a good husband and father? What kind of man are you?

Your responsibility is more important than your basketball accomplishments, because eventually your body won't let you play anymore, but you still have to live. Life goes on after the ball quits bouncing. What kind of concern do you have for others? This too is more important than basketball. If you are committed to excellence as a person, that will outlast your basketball ability and will come back to you.

The same attitude I put into basketball, I'm now putting into broadcasting. I watch tapes of all the games I broadcast, I search out advice from those I respect, I work on my weaknesses. The lessons learned from working as part of a basketball team are the same lessons in life. I encourage you to make a difference in your school, in your town.

My father was a great athlete and shared with me what he thought it took to be a super player. He told me that he played against Gus Johnson. I wanted to believe my dad, but Gus Johnson was a player I had watched on television and really respected, so I wasn't sure. As it turned out my dad and Gus Johnson did play against one another and when my dad and I ran into Gus, those two were like long-lost friends and talked about old times and games.

I ask you, can you listen to advice from your parents and coaches? Can you seek the words and ideas that will help you become a better person and player? When you leave your home at the beginning of the day, are you a follower or a leader? Do you have the courage to step out on the edge for the right reasons? Do you have the energy required to give your best at all times?

The other day we had a powerful storm in Indianapolis and one of the limbs of a tree in my yard was broken due to the wind, but was not totally broken off. It had been that way for several days before I went out and snapped it off. The leaves began to die within a few hours after that because it was no longer connected to its power source.

Are you connected to your power source, or are you broken off? Stay connected to your source of power — power from your God and the power you gain from learning. Learning takes place at all times if you are willing to put energy into it. My father was a police officer and made decent money, but we had a large family, so we had all the things we needed and only a few of the things we wanted.

When I was 16 years old I began selling insurance to make some extra money. One day I received my pay for selling the insurance and was feeling pretty good about myself. I was all set to go out and get my cheap car washed and waxed when my mother asked me if I had gotten paid, and I, of course, answered yes. She continued by asking me if I thought of sharing any of the money: "Forget about your father and me, have you thought about sharing any of your pay with your brothers and sisters, or have you only thought about yourself? I stood about 6-7 and weighed somewhere around 220 pounds at the time, but when my mother said what she did I felt about two feet tall.

What she said changed my life because I became more of a giving person from that day on. Do you have a willingness to give? Are you a giver of yourself? Are you a giver of your resources? If you are giving, is it possible for you to give more? This idea of giving can extend into basketball. Are you willing to pass the ball to an open teammate? Are you willing to set a screen and get somebody else open? Will you take a charge? Will you have a good attitude and be positive toward your coach and teammates if you are on the bench?

You can learn so many lessons through basketball. As a basketball player and as a student you need to understand your strengths and weaknesses and attempt to eliminate your weaknesses. Surround yourself with people that will challenge you in a positive way. The people who make you work are the ones who will make you better.

So, what kind of man are you and what kind of man do you want to be? Ask yourself these questions:

1. *Would you rather be respected or liked?* Anybody can be liked, but it is much more difficult and significant to be respected. To be respected, your actions must be consistently positive.

2. *What kind of attitude do you have?* What is your attitude toward basketball, homework, teammates? Are you a complainer or an encourager? What do you do when things don't go your way?

3. *What price are you willing to pay to develop as a student and as an athlete?* Are you willing to separate yourself from the many negatives of today? If a man was to try to ride two horses at the same time he could do it if they stayed side by side, but when the horses went in different directions the man could no longer ride them both. What horse will you chose to ride? You can't be an A+ student and a partier. Will you create destruction or production with your attitude and effort? What kind of man are you going to be? The type of man you are is far more important than the number of points you score.

4. *Will you apply the lessons you learn in sports to other areas of your life?* The basketball lessons and principles that you apply to hoops will build the foundation for your life. What is your game plan?

I wish you luck.

George Raveling is one of college basketball's greatest communicators, an outspoken man with worthwhile ideas. Raveling first gained note as a recruiter at Villanova and Maryland, and has been a successful head coach at Washington State, Iowa and USC. He was named the national Coach of the Year by several groups in 1992 when his USC team finished 24-6. His life extends well beyond the basketball court, however. He serves on several committees and advisory boards for the NCAA and other groups, and is one of the game's most respected and powerful voices.

★ George Raveling

As we begin, I think it is very important that we understand our role. Today, I am going to do the speaking and you are to do the listening. You have the most difficult job, because there is a big difference between hearing and listening. Listening involves understanding.

I'm going to tell you a story that I call "Page Four." Let's go back many years ago to a small town, on a hot and humid day. We cross a grassy field and come upon a playground and three young girls and a 20-year-old college student.

This group is going about the task of building an old western army fort out of popsicle sticks. A young boy approaches and he is troubled and confused, struggling to become the person he feels he can be, but he has no direction. He wants to talk and he asks the college student to listen, but that college student says to him, "Johnny I'd like to, but I have to finish this project. It's urgent. You understand, don't you, son? Could you come back tomorrow?"

The boy understands and says he will come back tomorrow. The next morning that college student is sitting, sipping a cup of coffee, reading the newspaper, and he turns to Page Four. I think I'll always remember that it was Page Four. I was that student, and a headline caught my eye that Johnny had committed suicide. Far too many nights in my life I hear a voice asking the Lord to let me please live that day over again.

There are situations all of us wish we could live over again. If I could talk to Johnny, I would say some of the same things I'm going to share with you today. You all play basketball, and many good things have happened in my life that started with a little round leather ball. Basketball gave me a chance to go to college because I could never have afforded it. It has given me an opportunity to travel all over the world and find out what I am capable of doing.

Everybody loves you right now because you can play that game of basketball, but one day they ain't gonna be there patting you on the back, so you'd better prepare yourself. If you beat Indiana on Tuesday night, does that make you a better person on Wednesday? If you believe that, you're a fool. I have met very many successful people, and the one thing they have all mastered is the fundamentals of winning in life.

The first thing you must do is to become a dreamer. It all starts with a dream, and for many of you, it is basketball. The problem isn't that we dream, it's that we don't dream big enough. Work at making it a reality, and then you will want to win at anything you do in life. Understand that it wasn't raining when Noah began to build the ark. Understand that there was nothing flying in the air except birds when the Wright brothers built the first successful airplane. Dreams can become a reality. We must dream big and work every day to achieve those big dreams.

Next, you need to be a learner. Wealth is not what we put in the bank, it's what we put in our brains. There's a saying that I like: Give me fish and I eat today, but teach me to fish and I eat forever. Your expectations should exceed all others. A great way to learn is to read, but do you know that 71% of all the books in the libraries are never checked out? Did you know that 51% of the people in America do not read a single book after their graduation? I challenge you to read one book a month. If you would read fifteen minutes a day for one year, you will read nearly 20 books. You become a learner when you are a reader. I set a goal to read 25 books during the course of a year several years ago. Now my goal is to read 86 books this year.

Our problems multiply much faster than our solutions. If we do not continue to read and do positive things with our time, we become part of the problems. However, there are 86,400 seconds in a day, and that gives us all the opportunity to be a little better person today than we were yesterday. I challenge you to ask yourself for 30 straight days the question: What did I do today to make myself a little better than yesterday?

Also, when was the last time you told your parents that you loved them? When was the last time you made a sad person smile? When was the last time you visited one of your former teachers? These are questions that make a difference in our society and make a difference in our character. The two simplest words in the English language are thank you — how many times do you use these two beautiful words. So, do you use your 86,400 seconds to build or destroy? To cause a smile or a frown? Do you believe in cans or cannots?

This leads me into my third major idea: Believe in yourself. The question for every day isn't what so-and-so thinks of you, but what you think of yourself. Right now in this room there is enough intellectual power to solve the world's problems. The problem is we don't believe that and most of us don't believe in ourselves. Surrounded by so much negative stuff in your life, maybe it is hard to believe you have depth and dimension, that you can do great things, but the human mind is very powerful.

Everybody sets their dial to success, but we turn it back toward failure with negative attitudes. Studies have shown us that most of "self talk" is negative. Whatever you put into the field is what will come up. It is the same with the mind. If you put negative ideas into your head, that's exactly what will come out of your mind. Everybody in this room is at least 25 percent better than they think they are and some are a lot better. You have got to say, "I'm the greatest!" Who knows more about you than you? You have to feel good about yourself if anybody else is going to feel good about you.

If all you players are just about the same athletically, what makes one team better than another? What makes one team win and another team lose? It's the mental attitude. You have to develop the mental skills along with the physical skills.

If it is to be, it is up to me! The harder I work, the luckier I get. A successful foundation for life starts with your attitude regarding yourself. I do understand it is difficult to be positive in our negative society and world. I realize that the first thing that happened to you in your life was that you got slapped. I know the first thing you did was cry. Why is there only one hour a day that is called "happy hour?" All the hours should be happy.

I know it's tough to be positive. We live in a society where the mailmen get paid more than the teachers. Seventy-five percent of the headlines are negative. It is tough to be positive, but we live in a place called America and we are Americans. The last four letters of American are *I can*. We can be positive and we can believe in ourselves.

Finally, you must set a game plan for your life. Establish a goal, believe there's a method for success and apply yourself to it. Remember, a goal isn't a goal until it is written down and posted. I write my goals down and post them by my bed and on my bathroom mirror, so I see them at the beginning and end of every day. If you don't have a goal, you don't have a game, and consequently you don't have any fun. Set goals, then you have a game and challenges, and then the fun really begins.

Along with these goals and with a game plan, you must be willing to work. Be a worker. You cannot keep your foot on first if you are trying to get to second. Everybody wants to get paid, but not many want to work. He who wants to work will find work, no excuses. My grandmother always told me that God provides for every bird, but He ain't gonna put food in their nests. It's the same with us. We gotta get out and work for it. Input equals output; if you give 25 percent, that's what you get.

It costs a lot of money to come to this camp. When you put your money down on something, to me that is making an investment. When you invest in something, you want a good return on your money. Getting a good return on your money may be to take the things you are learning here at camp and going home and working on your weaknesses. Don't just work on your strengths.

We can bring in all the greatest coaches in the game today and they can't make you into a good player — you have to make yourself into a good player. Sure they can tell you some things today and what you need to work on, but you have to do it. As great as John Wooden was as a coach, he wasn't the one who made all those players great. Bill Walton, Kareem Abdul-Jabbar, Sidney Wicks, Gail Goodrich, they had to do the work. Wooden could take Walton aside and tell him what to work on, but Walton could either take what he was told and embrace it or reject it. Luckily for Walton, he chose to embrace it. All any coach can do is tell you what it takes to be a player. Don't kid yourself, nobody can make you great but you.

Everybody in here can be great. If you're playing two days a week, you need to play seven. If you are working one hour a day, you need to work two. If you're working two, you need three. Somewhere out there in the boundaries of the continental United States, there is someone working four and five hours a day, seven days a week, that has equal ability to you, and at some point you are going to meet him head-to-head. He has the mental toughness, discipline, the conditioning, the attitude and when you meet him, who is going to break first? You, who has been working a couple hours a day, three days a week, or him who has been working four and five hours a day, seven days a week, every single day?

There are guys here with fantastic ability, but they'll never use it because they aren't willing to be successful. They won't do what it takes to use their God-given ability. I do believe that everybody here has the potential to be successful. I'm here to tell you that every one of you can be successful. See, practice is like putting money in the bank. If you don't put any money in, you aren't going to get anything out. If you put $100 in, you are going to get $100 out. If you $500 in the bank, you can get $500 out. The bank doesn't allow you to take out any more money than what you put in.

It is the same thing with life, and it's the same thing with practice. If you put a little effort into your life, you're going to get a little bit of results. If you put average effort into your life, you are going to get average results. If you put extraordinary effort into your life, you are going to extraordinary results.

That's how life works. Every one of you can be successful, but a lot of you don't want to be successful. You know why a lot of you aren't going to be successful in life? It is because you don't want to be. You hold yourself back. You are talking when you should be listening. You are daydreaming when you should be paying attention. You are busy chasing broads when you should be working. If I came to this camp with these great players and great coaches here, I would be trying to soak in as much information as I could, I tell you that. If some asshole was sitting next to me talking, I would tell him, "Hey buddy, shut up, will ya? I want to learn. This a chance for greatness. If you want to be a nothing, then you be a nothing. Don't talk to me about it."

But you know what? It takes guts to do that. It takes guts to stand up in a crowd and say, "Hey I've got to go, I want to go somewhere in life, I want to be somebody."

If you would ever take the handcuffs off yourself and let the success element enter in, you would be successful right now. Every human being dictates his own destiny. You are where you are because that's where you want to be. If you want to change it, stop programing yourself for negative reaction. God programmed everyone of you with the success element, but the only problem is that a lot of you haven't turned the machinery on yet. You guys are holding yourself back because you tell yourself that you can't do it. You tell yourself that you can't get good grades, that you can't do this or that. You have the wrong approach; you will never be successful with that approach, but you can change all of that. You have to open up your arms and let success enter into your body and into your minds. You have got to want to be successful. That's where it starts, you've got to want to be successful. A lot of you don't want to be successful. Oh, you think you want to be successful, but you don't.

See it is easy to be successful in this world, because 80 percent of the people don't want to be successful — all they want to do is to talk and daydream about being successful. There are a lot of people here who don't want to be successful, and 80 percent of the people you compete against in life don't want to be successful, and another 10 percent don't know how to be successful. So you are only going to compete against 10 percent of the population, and of the other 10 percent, five percent don't want to be the same thing you what to be.

Soon you will learn that it is easy to be successful. Psychologists tell us that the average human brain has more of an intellectual capacity than the five greatest computers every invented. They also tell us that no human being has ever used more than 10 percent of his brain capacity. The average human being only uses one percent of his brain capacity. One percent! We shut the rest off, we don't try to use it.

Did you know that the average champion in the athletic world is 5-10, 175 pounds? Just an average guy that was highly motivated. You don't have to be a big guy, you just have to have high motivation to be successful. God gave every one of you the ability to be a Jerry West, a Bill Bradley, an Oscar Robertson, or a Wilt Chamberlain. See, the problem is that a lot of you don't want to take advantage of the situations out there for you.

When those guys I just mentioned were growing up, there were no basketball camps. You guys are ahead of where those guys were at the same age. It wasn't until 10 years after I graduated from college that I found out that having your elbow under the ball had anything to do with the shot going in; that may have been why I couldn't shoot. There were no basketball camps out there for me; I still remember standing around the fence at the playground in Washington D.C., watching the old guys play, trying to learn how to play the game. I would watch guys like Elgin Baylor play at the playground and then go off by myself and work on the moves and shots I saw them do. Nobody was around to teach guys in my era how to play, but still guys like West, Chamberlain and Bradley became great.

You guys can become great too. There are guys sitting here right now saying, "There's no way I could be as good as Jerry West or Wilt Chamberlain." And that's where the problem starts, you are program-ing yourself for non-productivity. You are telling yourself that you can't be a superstar, but I'm telling you that you can. Jerry West's basketball camp was by a creek in Cabin Creek, West Virginia. Oscar Robertson's camp was in a ghetto in Indianapolis, Indiana. Wilt Chamberlain's camp was in an alley in West Philadelphia. They didn't have what you have, yet they became great. They started behind in the race, but they won. You can win too.

You have to remember that your success in life will be in direct proportion to the amount of effort that you put forth. What you do in your spare time is going to determine if you are going to be successful. Everybody in America practices two or three hours a day, everybody goes to work from 8 to 5, but the guy that becomes president of the company is the guy who works late hours. It is 5 o'clock, and he is still working in his office. It becomes 6 o'clock, and he is still in his office. It becomes 7 o'clock, and he is still in his office getting the job done. Pretty soon that guy starts moving up the ladder, getting things done. One day he becomes president because he was burning the midnight oil, putting in the extra effort, making the extra sacrifice, going the extra mile. He was doing the things that it takes to be successful in life.

I'm not telling you that basketball is the living end. Maybe you want to be a doctor, or a lawyer — whatever it is that you want to be in life, you ought to try to be the best at it. Never enter the contest, never enter the arena, unless you want to compete. The problem in our athletic world today is that it is divided into people who participate in athletics and people who compete. There are a lot of guys who are participants, but there aren't a lot of guys who are competing and putting out the blood, sweat, and tears that is necessary to rise above the crowd. Rising above the crowd is what you have to do.

Fellas, let's get this straight about success: success is not how much money you have, or how much property you own. Success is not whether you are driving a Ford or a Cadillac. A lot of people think that is success, but some of the most unhappy people I have ever met in my life had millions of dollars. To me, success is the logical progress of reaching a goal, and being the best at whatever it is you want to do. If you want to be a doctor, then try to be the best doctor. If you're the best doctor, it doesn't matter if you make $5 a week. There is nothing wrong with being a janitor, or a farmer, or a teacher. We have become a society where doing these things is somewhat of a disgrace; there is absolutely nothing wrong with doing these things.

What I am interested in is, if you enter the competitive arena, you compete and give it everything you have. When you walk off that court, did you give it everything you had, or did you save a little for tomorrow? When you walk off that court, are you exhausted, or could you have gone for another two hours? If you could have gone for another two hours, then you didn't give it everything. What are you saving it for? There might not be a tomorrow. Don't save for tomorrow, get it done today, then move on to something else tomorrow.

You can be a success out there. Some of you are going to change your life right now. You got to pick something out in life that you really like doing. It doesn't matter what it is. For me, I want to be a basketball coach. There is nothing in the whole world that I want to do besides coach basketball. If I got fired tomorrow, I would go out and be somebody's assistant coach. I love everything about being a basketball coach. I get up in the morning and I love going to work. Every day is a new adventure. It is exciting for me.

You need to find something in life that you want to do, something that you love. Here is the standard I use for determining what I should do: I want to pick something out to do that I would still do, even if they didn't pay me. That's the standard I use. If they didn't pay me and I could still get enough money for food, clothing and a house for my family, then I would still choose to coach basketball. If you don't enjoy what you are doing, you will never do a good job at it. So, find something in life you really enjoy doing.

As you start in this job or activity, don't depend on anybody else to get the job done. Something that I have learned the hard way is that if you have something that you really need to get done, then do it yourself. Learn not to depend on other people. Don't depend on luck. There is no such thing as luck. The only thing I know about luck is that it is unlucky to be behind at the end of the game. The only other thing I have heard about luck that I believe in is the saying that the harder I work, the luckier I get.

A lot of people are at the back door looking for a four-leaf clover, while opportunity is knocking on the front door. When opportunity knocks, it doesn't stay there very long, so you'd better be at the door and welcome it in. Don't be looking for luck. Don't be looking for somebody to make life easier for you. Row your own boat in life.

I am not that smart of a man, so I operate my life on a simple formula: input equals output. Whatever I put into my life, that is exactly what I am going to get out of it. That is just what is going to happen in your lives.

The other thing I want to point out to you is that I don't think I am better than you. See, I need this too. My life needs a lot of improvement too. There are a lot of things I haven't accomplished that I want to, but I want you to get a formula for success. Maybe it will be "input equals output." Or maybe it is the formula that "sweat + sacrifice = success." Most people today have some sort of success formula, something to keep them moving along. Find one that works for you.

So I leave you with these challenges: be a dreamer, be a learner, believe in yourself, and set a game plan that makes you be a worker.

Hubie Brown has been part of the Five-Star camp from the beginning, and has been one of the camp's instrumental figures as a coach and lecturer. Learning the ropes as an assistant coach at William & Mary and Duke, and then with the Milwaukee Bucks, he got his big break when he was named head coach of the ABA's Kentucky Colonels. He led them to a championship, then helped turn the Atlanta Hawks and New York Knicks into winners. He's now an NBA television analyst, but hasn't forgotten his Five-Star roots. He's recognized as one of the premier lecturers in the world.

★Hubie Brown

What we are going to show you today are the little things that make it happen. Give this a little thought: in 25 years there have been 35,000 guys in this camp. Think about it, 35,000, and only 150 have made it in the NBA. What are your odds? The key thing today, as a high school player, is to get a college scholarship, make the most of it for four years, and have your degree. Then, if you have the talent, you go to the NBA.

Today I want to show you some basketball things that I teach at the pro level. If you sit here and tune me out, you are a fool. I just came back from Spain where I worked with the top 15 players in Spain. I am going to show you the same little things that I showed them. Exactly the same things I taught when I coached professional teams in Kentucky, Atlanta, and New York. Little things that get you open.

Don't tell me you've got slow feet. Because when they vote for the best player who ever played the game, the guy who usually wins is Oscar Robertson. Oscar Robertson was 6-5, 225 pounds, and half a step slow. When you talk about Magic Johnson, you talk about a guy who is 6-9 and half a step slow. When you talk about Larry Bird, you talk about a guy 6-9 and half a step slow. Don't tell me you gotta be quick and blazing fast. You play with your head and then with your feet.

I just watched the semi-finals up on the courts today and I saw a lot of things happen up there on both courts where guys were getting smacked around. That shouldn't happen, if you know how to play. Imagine guarding a guy who is wanting to cut through the lane and you want to stop him. You cannot stop him by using your hands; he

107

will bust right through your hand. Just like when you are guarding a guy in the pivot, you can't defend with your hands on him. A man cutting or posting will go right through you. What you must use against a guy cutting through the lane on you is your forearm. So when you play basketball you never play with your hands down. You have to have your hands up, so when people cut on you, you can hold your position and not be moved.

Similarly, when a man is posting up, I use my forearm and put it across his back. When I use my forearm I am using my strength. I send a message to the guy I am guarding. There are only two or three guys refereeing, you have plenty of opportunities to use your forearm stuff. All week in camp, I see the downscreen happen and every time the offensive man pops out and comes to the spot. Regardless of what the defense did against the screen, the offense did the same thing. As a result the offense allowed the defense to dominate them.

Anytime the defender is tougher or quicker than you and he follows you on the downscreen, you must grab the jersey or shorts of your teammate who is screening for you. When the offensive player does this, the defender cannot get through the screen. It is not how fast I go, but how well I read my defender. If the defense switches, then I pull the new defender across the lane with me and the screener now has post-up position on the switching man. If he looks for the ball, he has a layup. My teammate gets a layup all because I am using my inside hand to grab my teammate and then take the switch defender across the lane. If the man guarding the offensive player setting the down-screen loosens up and creates space for the defender guarding the man receiving the screen, then the offensive man should still grab the screener and as he grabs he sees the defender jump to go through the screen. The offensive then pulls himself back and into the lane. If the defense switched, then again the screen can seal the switch defender and get a layup.

It is not how fast you go, it is how well you read the defender. You all know the bump. If the defender guarding the man receiving the screen goes through again, I bump my screener and the screener will drop step. As I fade, if the defense switches, I catch and bounce pass to the screener posting on the switch defender.

Too often I see the wing defender double down on the post in a manner so that he does not take away the offensive post player's middle or baseline move and at the same time he turns his back to his man on the wing. If the ball is passed from the post out to the wing, the man doubling down has to turn and run at the three-point shooting threat. You can eliminate this if the offensive player spots up and gives you a shot fake that takes the defender out of the play. If the defender runs by the three-point shooter, he allows him to readjust and take the uncontested shot.

You must become a smart defender. When the pass goes in, I go and double down in a position that takes away the offensive post man's middle move. This allows my post defender to get closer to his man and anticipate the baseline move. More importantly, the double down defender can see his man relocating on the three-point line. Now he runs, not by the shooter, but at his chest — this eliminates the effectiveness of the shot fake at the three-point line. By running at the three-point shooter's chest, he forces the shooter to dribble right or left. If the shooter is right-handed, the defender should run at his chest but shaded to the shooter's right side. Now, when the offensive player takes his dribble to the left he is no longer outside of the three-point line, and he does not have a clear path to create a two-on-one.

Why should this be an issue? I just watched the Five-Star NBA semi-final and a team hit three threes in the last minute to tie the game. All the three-point shots were created because the defender ran by the shooter on the shot fake and let him readjust and get off the shot. Sure they made the shots, but they could have been eliminated if the defender would have run at the shooter's chest.

So, No. 1, when you double team, you double in the lane, and No. 2, when the ball is passed out you run at the shooter's chest. So far you have learned to grab your teammate when he is setting a downscreen for you so that you are the boss over your defender. You double down in the lane to take away the post player's middle moves. You run at the shooter's chest when coming out of a double down to prevent the shot fake on the three-pointer.

The next thing that I saw watching the games today that we need work on is how to handle the trap. When the defense gets you in the trap and your coach is telling you to hit the open man, I know you want to toss him the ball and tell *him* to make the pass. I know what it is like, it isn't easy. Especially if you are coming in from the suburbs to play in the state championship with your all-white team. Your point guard doesn't want to come across halfcourt. He's saying, "Ah crap, not again!" And the coach, who doesn't know how to coach, is saying, "Make the pass, make the pass, hit the open man!"

You've all been in that type of situation. The only trouble is that the guy picking you up on defense is better than you. He's quick, he's dominating you. You want to go to the middle of the court, but he won't let you. You keep thinking, I gotta go over there, and he keeps making you go to the sideline, and at some point he might even spit on you and say some other words that aren't too good. He continues to chase you into the trap.

So, the first thing that you should never do is try to pass over the trap off the dribble, because the back guy in the defense will rotate and steal. I don't care what league you are playing in, you never throw over the trap off the dribble, because in order to get the pass over the defender it has to be a lob pass, which allows the defense to rotate and steal. So when I see the trap coming, I back up and make the trap come out. Now when they trap, it is four offensive players against three using the entire half court.

If you do get trapped and are forced to pick up your dribble, you must first take the trap low. When you take the trap low (bend your knees and move the ball to a low position) and the defender goes for the ball, you are all basically the same height. The worst thing you can do if you are trapped is to pick the ball up and put it above your head. The next-worst thing you can do is to try to pass the ball off the dribble over the defense.

What you always do is back the trap out and then you take the trap low. Then, keeping your low position, pivot side-to-side looking for the curl pass around the trap. As you step wide looking to curl pass around the defense, the defense will slide to the side so that it doesn't allow the curl pass. If the defenders are good, they will slide and prevent the curl and at the same time prevent the sharp pass over the top, and the hook pass over the top, by keeping their inside hand up. So the offense should take the trap low, pivot wide and low looking to throw the curl, then the hook. If nothing is open, then pivot to the other side of the trap and look for the curl pass, and then the hook pass, then step at the other defender and split the trap. As you split the trap, remember that you can pick up your pivot foot as long as you pass or shoot before the foot touches the floor.

The next part of basketball that has become so frequently used, but can be stopped so easily if you use the team concept on defense, is the pick-and-roll. The Detroit Pistons, when they were winning championships in the NBA, the pick-and-roll was their bread and butter. The pick-and-roll came in when Moses parted the Red Sea, but it still works because guys can't defend it.

If the man with the ball in the pick-and-roll set has no outside game but is a good dribbler, you force him to go off the screen on the top side. As he goes off the screen, you go below the screen and meet him on the other side of the screen. The man guarding the screener must get above the line of the screen and keep a hand on the screener so that if he goes to the goal you can stay with him, because you will know when he goes. If the man with the ball can't shoot, you do not follow and get picked off.

If you are guarding a good shooter, like a Joe Dumars, I cannot let him get to the middle of the floor. So when I hear my teammate call, "Pick left!" I immediately go to the top side of the screen and the man guarding the screener keeps a hand on the screener and plays him on the baseline side of the screen. You cannot let a scorer like Joe Dumars get to the middle of the court. So when the scorer with the ball then drives to the baseline side, you can trap with the man guarding the screener and the man guarding the ball who is coming from the top side of the screen. Trap the ball with those two and rotate to cover the screener with the other defenders.

One thing I have to mention that will help you greatly on offense if you are running the pick-and-roll is that you should never pick up your dribble after only one dribble off the screen. You should always take two dribbles to spread the defense out. I don't care if they switch or not, you always take two dribbles off the screen in the pick-and-roll. If you only take one dribble you will not get your pass to the roll man; the defenders are too big, and the pass will get stolen. Remember, two dribbles off the screen.

Now, imagine that I have just scored the last five times down the floor, and your coach is yelling at you while you're trying to defend me, "Don't let him get that first mark, don't let him get to that first mark!" So you stand on that first mark. All coaches do that — you hear 'em all the time saying things like, "Don't let him get to his spot." There are a lot of guys who will try to keep you from getting your spot. Guys like Bill Laimbeer will keep you from getting your spot. As you come down the lane, Laimbeer will wrap you in the head as a preliminary move to keep you from getting to your spot. We call that "non-contact, NBA style." I was an assistant coach in Milwaukee for two years with Jabbar. All those year Kareem was in the league, he would come down and every coach would scream, "Don't let him get his spot!" And there would be a chicken fight between Kareem and the guy who was guarding him, each trying to get to a spot. Nowadays everybody passes the ball, dribbles, cuts, and posts up.

I know there is a station here at camp that teaches how to post up, but I'm going to show you how to get to your spot. Everything I am showing you today works at the highest level of the game, the NBA, in the last two minutes of the game. If you think you are a man, you try to get down the floor to your spot in the last two minutes of the game, especially a finals game. You gotta be a man — none of that, "Ohhh, he hit me with an elbow." That happened in the first five minutes; now the whistle doesn't blow unless there is blood. The players decide the game, not the refs.

You step into the defender, pivot with your hands up so that they can't say you are hitting him, and you sit right down on his thigh. That's right, baby, I sit right down on his thigh and wiggle my way to my spot. My butt does the job. And for the guy who fronts you, you need to post on the first mark and then go up the lane. Trust me, the fronting defender will follow. After you take that additional step up lane from the first mark, put your forearm across his back and look for the ball. Don't tell me because a guy is fronted he is not open. Here, what's your name, son? Rasheed Wallace, and you're what, 6-9? So here's a guy 6-9 fronting me. Now I know this kid can play, and he's only a sophomore. But even with him fronting me, I'm still open if I take him up the lane, put my forearm across his back and go after the pass that is thrown to the corner of the backboard.

What kind of game do you have in the lane? A year ago a little guard from Division III who averaged 32 points a game made the Phoenix Suns, but he would go by his man and get into the lane and a 7-footer would be waiting for him. Isn't it amazing that you only have one-hundredth of a second to make a decision in the lane? The best at making this decision in the lane was a kid out of New York named Tiny Archibald. Tiny led the league in free throw attempts so many times it is amazing. He got down in the lane and could score with the baby hook, with the left or right.

Let me ask you a question, all you guards: where's your game? Two little guys that played when Tiny did were named Charlie Criss and Calvin Murphy. They would get into the lane and go at the big guy and then step back and jump back and hit the "J" over the big man. Can you do that? If I am small, I gotta have the hook and the step-back J. In taking the baby hook, you don't take the shot out of your chest, you take it out of your hip pocket. When you pick the ball up you pick it up off the dribble with one hand under it and the other on top of the ball and then you take it out and up. It is incredible how you can get it off against anybody. You practice the baby hook by starting in the middle of the lane and taking one dribble and shooting the hook with back spin on the ball. So, when you go by your man and meet up with the big guy, you know you can score because you are going to take the baby hook shot from out of your thigh or hip pocket with backspin. Or you are going to stop on a dime with your lead leg and step back and jump back and take the baby jumper.

I remember a few years ago Garf took me outside this gym and introduced me to a kid who Garf said was the best defender in America. So I go with Garf to meet this kid. The kid was about four feet tall, but his thighs were as wide as he was tall. His name was Muggsy Bogues. He said he was playing in 10 minutes on Court 3 right outside the gym against a guy named Pearl Washington. I said, "Pearl Washington, from Boys High in New York?" He said, "Yeah, that's him. Come watch me play."

So Garf and I went over to watch him. Shoot, everybody in the camp is bigger than Muggsy Bogues, but Muggsy can guard anybody. In the first quarter against the mighty Pearl Washington, he stole the ball five times and layed it up five times. I swear to God he did. He'd steal it and lay it in and sprint back and would be chopping his feet waiting for Pearl to come across the halfcourt line again. He simply kicked Pearl's butt. Muggsy couldn't shoot, however. He'd take a foul shot and it would hit the side of the backboard. Everybody said he couldn't shoot, but Muggsy didn't listen to the people who said he wasn't good enough. He could stop your best guard and take him totally out of the game. On offense, he would blow the ball up the court and make it happen, in high school and most of the time in college. But in the pros, he got into the lane and they backed off him and said, "Score, Muggsy." And his playing time went down, but because he played so hard he stayed around the league long enough to work on his game so that now he gets in the lane and can score, and now if he gets fouled he goes to the line and knocks 'em down.

I asked Magic Johnson during the first round of the playoffs this year if his association with Isiah Thomas was the motivation that causes him to excel. Magic said, "Hubie, Isiah and I are social. My motivation for 10 years has been going downstairs and getting my newspaper and immediately checking what Larry Bird did the last four minutes of the game — that's my motivation."

Did you know both Bird and Magic shot just over 70 percent from the free throw line in their first year? Then Larry Bird shot his 73, 78, 83, 80-something, then 90%from the line? All of a sudden Magic goes from the low 70s to the 80's to 90 to 91% from the line. Magic Johnson becomes one of the best three-point shooters in the league after not being able to shoot outside in his first six years. This happened after six and seven years in the NBA and two MVP awards. All of a sudden Larry Bird comes back with the lefty hook. Everybody says, "Oh no, Bird has another shot!" All of a sudden Magic Johnson comes back a year later and starts hitting baby hooks in the paint. These two guys have won MVP awards, and each year they come back with something new.

What are you going home from camp with that's new? You say, "I can blow by those guys in the AAU leagues." Hey, nobody guards in the summer. What happens when you go back to school? Back when this camp started, Boys High in New York had 6,500 boys in the school, and the basketball team kept 12. Think it wasn't tough to make the team there? Lenny Wilkins, a Hall of Famer, played one half of his senior year; he couldn't make the team. How would you like to have been at DeWitt Clinton with 9,000 boys, where only 12 make it? What do you think your chances would have been?

Don't tell me how hard you've got it, I want to know what you got. I showed you six different things today to give you something with the pressure on. Can you score in the lane? Do you understand that taking the hook from your hip instead of from your chest keeps you from getting it blocked? Do you understand the pin when a guy fronts you in the post? Do you understand how to attack the trap?

You are responsible for your own actions. Were you coachable this week, or did you have an attitude? They probably disciplined you here, so they probably took away your time. If you go back to school and you've got an attitude, they'll take away your time. They do the same thing in the NBA. You have an attitude, they take away your time, and in the pros they take away your money.

Let me ask you again, are you coachable? Did you take advantage of the week? My first week as an assistant coach at Duke, they sent me up to the Bronx. I go to watch this game, a Saturday afternoon summer high school game. One of the top three teams in America, Power Memorial, is playing Roosevelt High School at 3 o'clock in the afternoon. It is 90 degrees and it is my first assignment at Duke. I go to this playground. On Power Memorial they have Len Elmore, who played in the NBA 12 years. He's an attorney now and has his law degree from Harvard. And they have Ed Searcy, 6-7, who went to Duquesne and then to St. John's. In the backcourt, they have Jack Trembell. All three of those guys were at camp, all three had grades and could go anywhere in the country.

Someone there asked me who I was there to see, and I said I was there to see the three kids from Power. He said, "You're not here to see Joe?" I said, "Joe who?" He said, "Joe Hammond." I said, "Who's Joe Hammond?" He said, "Come on, Hubie, you're an old Jersey guy and you don't know Joe Hammond?"

Out comes this Roosevelt team and Joe Hammond. Hammond is 6-3, 140. Maybe 140 pounds. He was so skinny that when he turned sideways I was looking for the crack in the court to see where he went. Now, they were playing against the best team around and Joe Hammond gets what? 30? 40? 50? No, he gets 53 points, that's all. On Jack Trimbell, Ed Searcy and everybody else.

You all have heard of Len Elmore, but you haven't heard of Joe Hammond, because Joe Hammond never went to school. He was a pool hustler and a drug guy. He played in all the New York all-star games, and he was one of the greatest to come from the playgrounds.

I am asking you who you are in this story. To me, the five best players in the history of this camp are Ronnie Johnson, who 25 years ago out of Long Island University only took nine bullets in the back in a bank job, that's all. How about Donald Washington from St. Anthony's High School? He played for John Thompson at St. Anthony's. He was 6-8, a first team All-American, then went to North Carolina and nobody ever heard from him again. Mel Montgomery out of Buffalo, 6-5, there's not a better small forward in the country, I'm telling you that right now. How about Chris Washburn? Wow, what a tragedy!

You know what is important about them? They were all MVP's at Five-Star. Being MVP at Five-Star doesn't mean crap. Hey, we have seen some guys here at Five-Star. So you aren't impressing any of these coaches; they go down and have a couple of beers and laugh at your butt. Are you kidding me, we've been messed over by the best of you. See, I gave you five giants. You don't hear crap about them, because they don't have their priorities in order.

How about you? For all you guys that are too small, could you be Rick Barry, who was 6-2 in high school and grew to 6-7 in college? Or are you Dennis Rodman, coming out of high school with no place to go, mopping floors in the airport, and suddenly growing from 6-foot to 6-8 when you are age 19 and 20?

For all you guys who are being recruited heavily, do me a favor and don't take the money. The money is so small to go to a school that doesn't get you a degree, and they don't coach you while you are there. Those players might win a lot of games, but when they get to the NBA they go home fast because they are uncoachable, they don't know how to play. And most important, they don't have a degree. The life expectancy of an NBA player is three years. At 25 you are going to be here 50 more years. What have you got?

You are responsible for your own actions. Go down to your guidance counselor and find out if you're taking the right courses, find out what you can do to get that 700 on the SAT. Don't blame your coach.

So what is going to stop you from getting there, from making it? Five things. Write them down, they will be the key to the rest of your life.

One, low pain threshold. Remember Jabbar? Everybody would like to play 20 years in the league, but check how many games he missed. Outside of the year he broke his hand, check it out: 20 games, that's it. Michael Jordan is there every night, baby, getting double- and triple-teamed. Jordan just keeps coming. Jordan was also one of the most coachable kids to play at this camp. When the players in the NBA voted for who they wanted to take the last shot to win or lose the game, they voted unanimously for Jordan. Then they voted for who they wanted to be guarding the guy taking the last shot, and again they voted unanimously for Jordan. Is Jordan coachable? You bet he is.

Two, the great ones have a high basketball I.Q. for what the team is doing. Do you know all the plays? Do you know the defenses?

Three, you must be unselfish. If you are not unselfish you will be traded or you will be cut.

Four, are you willing to do the intangibles? What is an intangible? An intangible is Dennis Rodman taking a charge. How about Bill Laimbeer, who the fans hate, grabbing 15 rebounds in the fourth game of the championship series. Bill Laimbeer can't jump over that line, but in Game Five he gets 17 rebounds. You know where Bill Laimbeer was drafted? Do you know that nobody wanted him? He had to go to Europe for two years before he could get into the NBA. Then he came back and Cleveland didn't even want him, he was a throw-in on a trade to Detroit. Laimbeer said, "I can make a living being a tough dude, I don't have to be able to jump. I can take charges and do the little things for my team." Intangibles are diving on the floor, getting rebounds in traffic — intangibles!

And the last thing — drugs, alcohol, do you have them in your life? If you do, you aren't going to reach your potential.

What about you? Do you have one of these five? If you do, you aren't going to make it; you will not reach your potential. Here they are: low pain threshold, low I.Q. for the job, not totally unselfish, not willing to do the intangibles, not willing to give up the drugs or the alcohol. I then turn around and ask you, "Are you coachable? What did you learn from this camp?" And don't forget to thank the people who have helped you.

Rick Albro has long been one of Five-Star's most tireless teachers and lecturers. After 12 successful years as head coach at East Grand Rapids High School, he has been the head coach at Aquinas College in Grand Rapids for the past three seasons, where he's bringing a once-dormant program to life. Aquinas won seven games the year before his arrival. It has won 13, 18 and 16 since then, and he has been rewarded with the District Coach of the Year award twice.

★ Rick Albro

Don't assume. As the head coach of Five-Star this week I didn't assume that the camp would work hard and I didn't assume that the staff would work hard. I hoped that we would have a great week and we have, but I could not allow myself to assume, take for granted, that everything would go well. All that I could do is set an example of working hard. Everybody has the capability to set a good example.

If you can pick up just one thing or look at an issue in a different way, then this week has been a success. Some of you will hear everything I say, others have already turned me off. Maybe they have turned me off because I'm not a big name like Bob Knight, who spoke here in this same room not long ago, I don't know. If you haven't turned me off, then I am going to try to give you something that will make this week even more of a success for you.

I am not going to assume that you are going to listen to every word I say. I am also going to encourage you to not assume. If you break the word assume down, it looks like *ass u me*. When we assume, we make an ass of you and me. We all assume too much. We take our health for granted until we are sick. We take our parents for granted until we are away or they are gone. In fact, how many of you will let your parents know how much you appreciate coming to Five-Star? We unfortunately assume that the money to pay for camp comes easily.

You've probably heard the story of the Detroit Lions' football player who was paralyzed during a game, and the other player for the Lions who was killed while doing yard work. Don't assume — life is too fragile.

How do I keep going? I keep going because of individuals like some of you. It only takes one thing to keep me going, someone appreciating my effort. One person saying thank you will keep me going for a long time. Do you understand that your coaches love you? The reason they jump on you and yell at you is because they love you. They don't need to get worked up and go crazy. They do it because they care about their players, that is why they are tough on them.

At Aquinas we have open gym, just like a lot of you have at your high schools. Your coaches take their time to open the gym for you. Do you know what this open gym really is? It is a basketball party to get you better. That's right, it is a party where you get to do something that you enjoy doing and you get to do it with your friends who also like playing. It is a party. Now I encourage you to not only show up at the party, but show up with a purpose. Make that purpose be to get better. Get better every single day.

I have a question for you, and I want you to look deep within your own heart for the answer: What do you see? Do you like who you are? If you do like what you see, then good; however, if you don't like what you see then I've got good news. Tomorrow is a new day. You can change for the better and begin to feel good about who you are and what you stand for.

I would like Andre Patterson to come up front. Andre is a super player, one of the best rising juniors in America. He's 6-foot-9 and has all the talent to be a big-time Division I star. Here Andre, catch this basketball. What can that basketball be for you? It can be a lot of things for you. It can be an education, money, an occupation. That hunk of leather can be almost anything you want it to be. Through these next vital years, I hope that Andre can continue to be the quality person that he is right now. Don't assume that it will happen, you have to work for it everyday.

A lot of you have the talent to be a great player, but don't have a feel for the game. You don't understand the important concepts. I have five questions that I believe are the basis of being a great player.

1. Are you fun to play with? Do you appreciate your teammates enough to say "nice pass," or "my fault?" A lot of players play like the basketball court is on a slope. Uphill going back on defense and downhill going to offense. You are not fun to play with if you don't play hard all the time. If you don't play hard, why play? If you were picking up a team, would you honestly pick yourself based on how you play? Everybody has the potential to improve and become more fun to play with, if they improve their attitude.

2. How many things have you stolen? I don't mean how many things you've stolen from a store. I mean how many things have you stolen with regard to ideas and tips from coaches and other players. Just about all my basketball knowledge was taken from somebody. Don't be afraid to steal. Steal ideas to make you a better player and person and take those ideas home. Make those tips work for you. When you stop learning you stop growing.

3. Do you make other people better? If you are a point guard, do you pass the ball? Do you set an example of working on your game during the breaks at practice? In my many years of coaching I have seen about five guards who really make everybody on the team better. Average players play from the top of the key to the other top of the key. Good players play from the dots in the foul lane to the dots of the other foul lane. Great players play from baseline to baseline. Do you talk the talk or do you walk the walk? A lot of people talk like they are a team player until the time comes for them to actually give the ball up or spend time after practice. If you don't walk the walk, you won't make the other players on your team better.

4. Are you willing to do whatever is required? One of the greatest players I ever coached was named Garde Thompson (who went to the University of Michigan). He was a fantastic athlete. He could have been a super NBA player, but he didn't have the work ethic of a super star. You have got to pay the price for greatness. Nobody ever got hurt chasing a dream and not getting it. As John Wooden once said, "Success is piece of mind, which is a direct result of knowing you did your best in trying to become the best that you are capable of becoming." Don't be afraid to take a risk. Garde Thompson was as good as any player in the NBA at going to his right, but he couldn't go left nearly as well. Because he had great natural ability, he was able to get by without developing his left hand. When he moved up against the better players, however, he needed that left hand and he didn't have it. He didn't do what was required. You need to practice and play as if this were to be your last day; don't be the one who says, "I wish I would have done it in a very different way."

5. Are you a lucky guy? I didn't work Five-Star to have a fun week in the sense that a lot of people view fun. I worked camp to work hard. It is hard work to love somebody or something. The divorce rate is nearly 70 percent now because people are not willing to work. Your grades are lower than they should be, I would bet, because your grades are not a priority in your life. I hope that when you're 43 years old you'll have as much fun as I do. Working hard is love.

You all have good health, and you all have love from somebody that helped you get to camp. Everybody in this room is pretty lucky. When I was the coach at Grand Rapids High School in Michigan we had a great tradition. We had won 60 state championships at the school. We had great players in our basketball alumni — guys like Garde Thompson and Jim Boylan who went on to play major college basketball. Only a few of the great players played varsity basketball four years though.

We did have one young man who was going to have a chance to play four years of varsity basketball, but one day he was taking a shower and lost his balance and put his right leg through the glass shower door. It was a brutal thing. His thoughts went from playing four years of varsity basketball to whether or not he was going to make it through the night to see the next day due to the loss of so much blood.

We take so much for granted. We assume way too much. This basketball is not only a ball to me, it is a way of life. I hope that you have a purpose in your life. Make your time quality time, and always with a positive purpose.

Like most "overnight sensations," Mike Fratello worked long and hard to make it as a coach. After working as a college assistant at Rhode Island, James Madison, and Villanova, he joined Hubie Brown's staffs with the Atlanta Hawks and New York Knicks. He took over as the Hawks' head coach in 1983, and won 50 games or more four times. He was named the NBA's Coach of the Year in 1986, and his team won its division title and set a club record by winning 57 games in '87. After a stint in broadcasting, he is a head coach again with the Cleveland Cavaliers.

★ Mike Fratello

Five-Star is known throughout the country, and by coming to Five-Star people know that you are interested in receiving the best teaching you can get. It shows what you are about. Those who want the easy road and want to be given special things because they have a big reputation will not come to Five-Star — it is too demanding. You have to make your breaks here, just like you do in the NBA.

So, I ask you, what are you doing here and what do you want to get out of this week of camp?

You need three things to be considered as an NBA or major college player today. The first thing is shooting. If you're a shooter, they'll always find a place for you, but don't believe it's Easy Street. When I was coaching for the Hawks, one summer Doc Rivers, a very established player, and Roy Marble, one of our draft picks, worked out to develop the strength and flexibility we told them they needed. Every day they did stretching exercises, worked with the medicine ball, and worked out on the stationary bike, and then took a thousand shots. Those guys are in the NBA. Are you better than them? Are you willing to work as hard or harder than them?

The second is dribbling. At the higher levels your game comes off the move. You need to be able to go off your dribble to a place where you can get your shot. Let me tell you a story about getting your shot. For a long time, guys like Doc Rivers and Spud Webb and Dominique Wilkins took it personally when someone like Robert Parish or Bill Walton or Kevin McHale blocked their shot. Those guys were used to taking the ball underneath and pounding it through the basket.

It's not like that in the NBA. I remember Dominique, in one game against the Bullets, getting his shot blocked something like 16 times by Jeff Ruland and Manute Bol. He'd go inside and try to double pump and hook dunk and Ruland and Manute would just stand there and swat it. Manute is a kick. He loves talking junk to guys. They'll come in and he just stands there and says, "Take that stuff outta here!"

Well, Wilkins and the others finally got the message that they had to give those guys some respect. They started to develop their middle game, their in-between game from eight to 12 feet and even further, out to 15 feet. They did this by improving their handle. From there, they could make the defense commit and then go jam it down their throats. Without a handle they cannot do it.

The third thing you need is to be a thinker. Thinkers make good decisions on the court. You can't play the game at the higher levels unless you know how to think basketball. You have to know what you're capable of doing and do it the best you can. There are two categories of players in the NBA: specialists, guys who are very good at one or two things, and skill players, guys who are solid all-around. Think about what you are and play to your strengths.

These past few weeks I have been lucky enough to be around the Dream Team in Portland as they played for the right to go to the Olympics in Spain. What I saw that was so special was the truly great players of our time willing to submerge their egos. They made a commitment to agree to leadership and followed them with the ultimate goal being to win a gold medal.

Great players have challenges for themselves and they set them daily. Jordan in the Portland tournament started out with the goal of not letting his man score, but after a game or two he changed his goal to not letting his man get a shot off! The intensity he showed in attempting to achieve this goal of not letting his man get a shot off was amazing.

Your goals this week should be to understand how to make yourself into a player that can pass, dribble, and shoot; there are very few people that can do all three things well. Doc Rivers really doesn't have a left hand that is nearly as effective as his right. Hakeem has two moves and works on them only. I asked him when we were making a commercial together why he didn't learn two or three more moves. His response was, "Nobody works with me." At that I was amazed. Don't ever blame others for not teaching you — teach yourself. We all have access to film — watch Kevin McHale's up-and-under move; break it down and go work on it. Ask for coaching. You can always make yourself better, if you have a desire to improve and the energy to look for the materials and teaching.

When Dominique Wilkins came into the league he had no left hand, he shot in the 60 percent range from the free throw line, he had no handle in transition to get himself to the rim so that he could use his jumping ability. His first year in the NBA he averaged something like 17 points and shot 68 percent from the line, and nearly led the league in turnovers. However, he went to work on his game. He worked on his mid-range jumper, he improved his range, he spent countless hours on his handle and handle in transition, and made a personal commitment to improving his free throws. After averaging 17 points per game in his rookie year, he went to 28 points a game and then to 31 points a game. And his free throw percentage has gone from 68 percent to 82 percent. You can do it on your own — no excuses, men.

We all want to look like pros, we want to drive cars like the pros do, we want to dress like the pros, but we don't want to work like the pros do. In getting ready for the Olympics, Magic Johnson dedicated himself to being ready to win a gold. His daily schedule was to wake up at 5:30 a.m., start weight training for an hour-and-a-half at 6:30, and then take a nap. At noon he would shoot for an hour and 15 minutes. He ate lunch at 1:15, and then played five-on-five from 5:30 to 7:30. The next day he would do it all over again.

He works like a pro; very few people are willing to go through a schedule like that day after day. That is why there are so few that become professional athletes. Michael Jordan was a great athlete, but it was his dedication to weights and a better understanding of the game that got him his first championship ring.

Being around the Dream Team was such a positive experience for me. Seeing the game's greatest players working together without a concern for personal glory, only team success, is something I will never forget. Seeing Magic, Jordan, and Bird sacrifice is a lesson to each one of you. People don't understand that it wasn't just the players who submerged their egos for the Olympics. The coaches did as well. Chuck Daly was the head coach, but guys like Lenny Wilkins (who has one of the highest number of wins in NBA coaching history), Mike Krzyzewski (head coach of Duke's national championship teams), P.J. Carlesimo (head coach of Seton Hall) were all assistant coaches. They all were willing to play a role in the team's success. They wanted to contribute, they didn't care about recognition.

The coaches and players all said the best thing about being involved with the Olympic team was working with each other. Competitors understand that winning is the ultimate.

The Dream Team also found out that you have to be ready to play every game. The group of college players beat the Dream Team in the first scrimmage, but the next time they played it was a joke. The Dream Team destroyed them. They put it together and made a commitment to winning. They submerged their egos for the sake of a team goal, a gold medal for the United States.

You will remember Five-Star for the rest of your lives. Take advantage of what you have here at Five-Star, the competition, the teaching, the friendships. One week of camp will not turn your game around, but it will put you in the right direction. I hope that you can be the guy everybody on the team can rely on. I hope that you are able to trust and share. Please, don't let your ego make you think you are better than you really are.

Also, be sure to appreciate the things your families try to do for you. I remember overhearing Doc Rivers and Isiah Thomas talking once about their sons. It was after Dominique Wilkins' All-Star Game and they were in the shower soaping up. I happened to walk past and I heard them saying how it wasn't until they were grown up that they realized how smart their own parents had been, that it was incredible that so much of what their parents had told them was right. There they were, stars in the NBA, and it finally hit them.

LSU's Dale Brown has a well-deserved reputation for getting the most out of his talent. He has taken two underdog teams to the NCAA Tournament's Final Four, in 1981 and '86, and his '86 team is the lowest-seeded team (11) ever to make it to the Final Four. He's also coached four teams into the final eight, and has 17 consecutive non-losing seasons and 10 straight NCAA Tournament appearances. Brown, who has coached the Tigers for 21 seasons, has won four SEC championships and been named the conference's Coach of the Year four times. The underdog has become a top dog.

★ Dale Brown

I know that you don't want to be preached to on this closing day lecture, because I know I wouldn't want to be preached to. But I do have something that I came here for, and I hope you will let me steal a few of your minutes.

There is no one in this room — and it doesn't matter what your geographical background, your social background, your race, your religious background, or your economic background is — who isn't searching for the same thing. We are searching for peace, love, happiness and success. Most of us don't know how to find it; we wander around like a bunch of molecules. Right now there are molecules in this room; they bounce off that wall and off my big forehead and off the ceiling. You can't see them, but they are here and they are active. Most of us wander through our lives that way.

The sad thing is that there is so much greatness in this room right now. Eliminate basketball — some of you will be great, some average, some poor, it doesn't make any difference. There is greatness inside of you. The good Lord doesn't make any junk, man. If you are like me, and I bet there are some people like me out there, the reason that I feel I can talk to you is that when I was three days old my father left my mother. She called home from the hospital and he wasn't there. She had four dollars in her purse and she took a taxi home to that one-room apartment. I never saw my father until I was a senior in high school.

Thank God a camp like this one let me realize that I could find happiness and that I could be successful. I grew up with a chip on my shoulder, kind of looking to whip my father, although I had never seen him, and my mother was ill and we lived in a one-room apartment above a bar and a hardware store. She couldn't work, so we lived on her welfare check of $42.50 a month. And every month Ward County Welfare sent a check and at Thanksgiving and Christmas the Salvation Army and welfare agencies would bring chickens and turkeys and fruit. I never ate any of it.

But thank God one person touched my life, and he told me, "Dale, if you want something in life, fix it in your mind and go after it." Believe me, please, you can go to the top.

Now, what's life about? If we were to go on a journey, let's say to Tahiti, we would prepare for that journey with compasses and the other things that we would need. Yet, we are on a journey of life now. There are five billion of us bumping around in the world. Life is really a race, but a different kind of race. Really, it is set up with four major hurdles to overcome, and it doesn't matter how old you are or how many years you have coached, of if you are Jewish, Baptist, Yankee, Southern, or whatever, we all have to somehow get over these four hurdles. Once we negotiate those four hurdles, at the end of that race is a gold medal. That gold medal is what I said we all want: peace, happiness, love, and success.

Now we all have to come into our blocks and start this race. But life's four hurdles aren't so easy to get over. If you deny that they are there, pretend that they aren't there, then you know what is going to happen? You are going to live with a chip on your shoulder. You are going to be in the unemployment line, you will be living in poverty your whole life, and you will be unhappy. But if you just focus on clearing these four hurdles, you will be amazed at what you can do.

Let me tell you about the four hurdles. The No. 1 hurdle you have to get over in life is "I can't. What can little old me do? I grew up in a little one-room apartment, what can I do? I'm too poor. My mother's a hooker. There's no possible way I can make it in life." That's the first hurdle, and I am going to come back and help you negotiate it in a minute.

Hurdle No. 2 is being afraid to fail. Some people don't want to try to be great as a person, as a human being, as a basketball player, or as a student, because they say, "What if I fall flat on my face?" I would say, "Welcome to the world." The biggest successes in the world have probably failed the most.

Hurdle No. 3 is handicap. Man, I have heard 'em all; we have all got them. "I've only got one arm or one lung, this damn old society, you get shafted if you are this color or this race or this religion." All kinds of handicaps.

Hurdle four, this is one that many of us don't get over. You know, in a hurdle race all the hurdles are set up the same distance apart, the same height. You've seen them, guys like Edwin Moses, get over a hurdle and he knows that it is so many strides until another hurdle. But the last hurdle in this race of life is not the same distance apart, and it's not the same height and it is at an angle and it is the one most of us screw up. You don't need a mother and father to make it in the world — yeah, it is a lot easier. You don't need to be born with a silver spoon in your mouth.

If you can get over this hurdle, you can find peace, love, happiness, and success. It is called knowing yourself — knowing who you are, where you are going, and what you want out of life.

Let's go back to hurdle No. 1. Again, thank God that I was at a camp, because I was insecure, I didn't have a dad and we didn't have anything. I would crawl around theatres and pick up popcorn boxes — this is the honest truth — and put those boxes in my shoes because I had holes in my shoes. I never slept in a bed of my own until I was 22 years of age. My mother had a bed that pulled out from the wall and I slept on a couch about a foot from her for 21 years. Yet someone told me that I could make it in life.

Whenever I think that I can't do something, I think of several things. I think of a blind kid that I met at a summer camp in Leesville, La. I was giving a speech much like the one I am giving you now and I was walking back to my car and I heard footsteps. A blind kid with long blond hair and a white cane comes up to me and says, "Coach Brown, my name is Allen Lafife and I am from Mansfield, La., and I believe in your speech and I am going to go to LSU this fall and I am going to major in music and I am going to be one of the greatest drummers in the history of the world, thank you." And then the kid walked off and I was feeling kind of bad. I wondered as I drove home if I had really helped the kid or if I had half-conned the kid.

Three months later, let me tell you what happened. A receptionist calls me and says, "There is a young man here to see you and his name is Allen Lafife." I said, "Oh yeah, that's that blind kid with long blond hair." So I go out in the hall to see him. Now the receptionist's desk is a long way down the hall, and as I go to my door I hear this popping noise. Just as I open the door he says, "Coach Brown, it is great to see you, man, it is great to see you." "See me," he said that twice.

He came into my office and I noticed he didn't have that white cane. I said, "Allen, I don't want to be too nosey, but what was that sound you were making down the hall?" He replied, "Coach, after I heard you talk up there I made up my mind that I can do anything. And I went home and I was reading a book about bats and birds and I read that bats send out a sound, and I have developed a sound that lets me feel when I am by brick, wood, and so on. I can feel that when I am near another human being the sound comes back to my ears differently. The receptionist told me that your office was five doors down to the left, so when I was coming down the hall, every time I got the echo back off a wood door I knew that your door was this one."

Man, did that fire me up! He went to LSU and graduated with honors in music, but the week before he graduated he called me and asked me if I knew where the town of Gonzales, La. was, and where the gas station and grocery store on the corner was? I knew Gonzales because of a former player of mine named Fess Irvin. Well, he wanted to know if I could meet him there at 10 a.m. the next day, because he had a surprise for me. I said that I would be there.

So I get there, and he is waiting for me in a pickup truck with a guy and he waits until I get in the pickup and we are driving near an open field and he says, "Coach, I want to thank you for making me believe in myself. This is a surprise for you." Sitting in the open field is an airplane. I am thinking, What in the world is an airplane doing here? To end this story, Allen Lafife became only the fourth blind person in the world and the youngest blind person ever to sky dive. Imagine that handicap. Whenever I get down I think of him.

You have heard the story of Johnny Weismuller, of him getting that gold medal in the Olympics and what a stud he was, so much of a stud that he landed the Tarzan role on television. Yet years later 13-year-old girls would shatter his records. Today in Santa Clara, Ca., in a competitive swim club coached by Coach Hayes, every 13-year-old girl has not only broken the records of Tarzan, Johnny Weismuller, they have shattered them.

You know why? At 5 a.m., he gets those young girls in the meeting room and tells them to fix in their mind the idea that whatever you fix in your mind, you become. The French call it *idee fixee*. That's not bull, that's not conning you; remember it — *idee fixee*. He's got little 10-year-olds in at 5 in the morning and he tells them to think world record, world record, world record. So, these kids go out and they jump into the water and they are thinking world record, world record and you know what they do? They shatter world records. They can't make

trophies quickly enough for the world records that they are breaking. It is called *idee fixee*.

And, finally, don't think you can't do something because you are too dumb. Man, I used to think I was dumb. I didn't know what I could do. But I found out that the greatest muscle you have is not your bicep, or any of your other major muscles, the strongest ounces in your body are the eight-and-a-half located in your cranium called your brain, and the 10-and-a-half located behind your sternum called your heart.

If you add them together it equals 19 ounces. Those 19 ounces are going to dictate your success. If you think that you are going to be a bad dude and say, "Yeah, I ain't going to make it in life, yeah man, my dad's an alcoholic, yeah man, I got screwed on my team," that's what will happen, because you are making an excuse for not succeeding.

Whenever I think that I can't do something, I think of this guy. There's a record, and you guys have probably never heard of it; it's called the dead backlift. What you do in this event is lift a certain amount of weight and walk with it a certain distance. The record for dead backlifting was 4,230 pounds; it was set by a French-Canadian in 1896.

In 1957 a young man broke that record, and I want to tell you about him. His name is Paul Anderson, and he grew up in Georgia. As a boy he was fat, sick, and he had a liver problem. When he was five years old, his mother gave him some crayons. They were a poor family. She told him, "Don't you lose these crayons, your daddy worked hard for the money to get you these crayons."

Paul went to school in a one-room school, and one day during recess some of the big, tough guys grabbed his crayons and broke them, threw them in the grass, pushed him in the face and then they ran off and laughed. Paul Anderson said right then, "So help me God, I am going to be the strongest man in the history of the world so that I can stand up for what is right."

That was a bunch of bull, right? A little fat kid from the hills of Georgia? Well, he started to develop and became the strongest in the one-room school house. Then he went on and won the Georgia weightlifting contest. Then he won an Olympic weightlifting championship. He was so good that when the Russians and Bulgarians, who were the best at that time in weightlifting, had to drop out, that's when he started competing. He went out and shattered all the records.

But what he did in 1957 in Melbourne, Australia is unbelievable, men. Remember the record for the dead backlift was 4,230 pounds. Paul Anderson got under a weight of 6,235 pounds — that's two tons! No man had even broken the old record at the time, and he lifts 6,235 pounds. You know why he was able to lift that fantastic weight? It was because he fixed in his mind at five years old, while laying on his butt with his crayons broken, that he was going to be the stongest man in the history of the world.

Hurdle No. 1, saying "I can't," we got over. Hurdle No. 2, remember, is being afraid to fail. I didn't understand what this meant for a long time. You can't be afraid to fail. But it is just like when you are coming to Five-Star all your friends say, "You are going to Five-Star? You are going to get killed!" Or you say, "I am going to be a good student," and your friends tell you, "You fool, you don't have a chance at being a good student." Well, if you keep beating it into your head that you don't have any brains, you are going to start to believe it. All of us have self doubt, no matter how confident we seem. Hey, God doesn't make any junk, you all have brains and ability.

If you are afraid to do something you are never going to make it. A guy named Bob Richards was a great decathlon and pole vault champion. He used to be on the front of the Wheaties box. You guys are too young to remember him, but he was a great motivational speaker. One time he told me, "Dale, it is not your I.Q. that matters, it is your F.Q." I said, "Bob, I understand I.Q., but what is this F.Q.?" He said, "F.Q. is your failure quotient. How much failure can you take."

You know how most of us handle failure? We get kind of embarrassed, we start to feel inferior, and we start to doubt ourselves. To help me over hurdle No. 2, I often think of baseball players. Before Hank Aaron broke the home run record, Babe Ruth had the most home runs, but do you know the leading failures in baseball, the guys who struck out more than anyone else? I'll give you some of them: Babe Ruth, Hank Aaron, Reggie Jackson and Mickey Mantle. These guys struck out more than anybody who ever went to the plate. Now can you imagine if these guys were afraid to go to the plate to bat?

By the way, do you know how Hank Aaron became the home run champ? He must have listened to *idee fixee*, because when he was nine years old he was listening to a World Series game with his mother and a guy hit a home run and the announcer said that that home run would be heard around the world. Little nine-year-old Hank turned to his mother and said, "Someday, I am going to hit a home run that will be heard around the world." And he did it.

Now, imagine he had been up to bat four times and struck out his last time up, and he says, "No, I'm not going up there to bat, send Garfinkel, I just struck out." No, he didn't say that. He went up there and said, "Come on, I know I can do it," and he knocked it out, all because he wasn't afraid to fail.

I just came back from Moscow. I was at the Goodwill Games, and the night before I left to go to Spain for the world basketball championships I had the opportunity to spend about an hour with Bill Russell. He was doing the color with Rick Barry in the World Games. I said, "Bill we have never talked about this, but I recruited a player out of your high school in Oakland, Ca., named Dave Williams. Is it true, like he told me, that you were cut from the high school team as a junior and that you were a substitute halfway through your senior year. He said, "Let me tell you the story. I went out for the team twice in junior high, and both times I was cut. My junior year of high school I went to try out and the coach told me I was probably wasting my time, that it was embarrassing for me, that I should just forget about basketball."

Bill Russell just told me this in Moscow a few weeks ago! Well, Bill hung in there and made the team his junior year, but hardly ever played. But the rest is history now. He played for the Boston Celtics and won all those world championships, and it goes on and on and on.

I don't know if you know these people; I'm not trying to impress you with my intelligence, but every time I fail I think of two men. How would you like to be this guy: a sculptor, a painter, a scientist, a biologist — this guy was brilliant. The guy invented the submarine 500 years before it became operational. He was so scared that they were going to burn him on a cross because they thought he was a witch or something that he hid the drawings of the submarine. Five hundred years later they find the drawings. The man's name was Leonardo DaVinci. Brilliant man. In his autobiography he said, "Ninety percent of all my solutions have been incorrect." Ninety percent wrong! Einstein, who many call the greatest mathematical mind to ever live said, "Ninety percent of all the problems I tried to solve, I couldn't." Somehow, these guys hung on and were not afraid to fail.

Well, here's what is happening to a lot of you. You got over hurdle No. 2, being afraid to fail, but you're like me; you're a procrastinator in some ways. You say, "Well, he has some good ideas, I'll start when I graduate." Or, "I'll wait until January 1st." That's called procrastination, and I'll tell you a little story.

The devil wasn't getting enough people to go to hell, so he called a meeting of all the devils in the world and he told them to meet in hell and to come with an idea how they could get more people in hell. There are five billion people in the world, and he wanted to get them all. So, they all came to the meeting and they parked their pitch forks at the door. They start the meeting and the first little devil said, "Satan, I think I know how we can get more people in hell. Let's tell all the people that there ain't no hell." Satan said, "Sit down, man, those people are smarter than that, they are suffering right now, they know there is something worse coming." The second little devil stands up and says, "I know how we can get more people to hell, Satan, let's tell 'em there ain't no God." Satan said, "We've tried that for years, and man just knows that there is something bigger out there, a supreme being watching over them." The meeting went on and on and they weren't getting anything accomplished, when finally this one devil stood up — and I wish he never would have said anything, darn him — the smallest devil of all walked up to the front and said quietly, "I think I know how we can get these people to hell, let's tell them there's no hurry." Satan said, "What did you say?" The little devil repeated, "Let's tell them that there's no hurry." Satan said, "That's a marvelous idea, everybody go out and spread the word to the entire world that there's no hurry, and they will screw up!"

Well, ever since that meeting, over the gates of hell there is a sign that's illuminated and it says, "Standing Room Only." Hey, man, it is filled up, baby. So when you think that you will start tomorrow, think again and don't procrastinate.

And I don't think you are dummies, by the way. I think you also have enough brains to figure that out. Before we get to hurdle No. 3, I want to tell you a story Bob Richards told me. A football and a basketball coach were arguing about who the stupidest guy was. The football coach was sitting in his office and he says, "I have got this tackle on my football team who is the stupidest guy I have ever met, you can't believe it. Here he comes, don't say anything, I'll show you how dumb he is." This guy comes walking in, he's about 6-9, 280 pounds, his shoulders hit the door when he tries to come through the doorway. The football coach says, "Hello, Roger, hey I want you to do me a favor. Take this quarter and go on downtown and buy me a Cadillac." The football player says, "OK, Coach!" Boom, boom, boom, he walks away. The coach says, "Can you believe that guy?" The basketball coach says, "He's dumb, but I got a guy on my team that's even dumber." No sooner did he say that when this 7-1 guy walks in and hits his head on the doorway and says, "Hey, Coach, how ya' doing?" The basketball coach replies, "Great, Randy, I'm doing great. Hey Randy, do me a favor will ya', run down to my office and see if I'm there." The basketball player says, "OK, Coach!" Well, the coaches are shaking their heads thinking about how dumb their players are. Meanwhile, the football player and the basketball player meet up with each other waiting for the elevator. The football player tells the basketball player, "I've got the dumbest coach in the country, he gave me a quarter to go downtown to buy him a Cadillac and he didn't even tell me what color he wanted." The basketball player says, "Well, that's nothing, my stupid basketball coach is sitting up there on the third floor with your football coach and tells me to go on down to his office and see if he's there. Well, the stupid jerk, he had a phone right there, he could have called to see if he was there."

So I don't think there are any of those guys here. Anyway, hurdle No. 3. I used to hate it when a teacher would ask you to raise your hand. The teacher would say, "If you brushed your teeth, raise your hand. Or if you had fun today, raise your hand." Well, when they cut my umbilical cord I decided that I wasn't going to raise my hand to answer questions. So, don't raise your hand to answer, but I am going to ask you a question. How many of you guys in this room are making up their minds that they don't want to find peace and happiness? There are guys out there already making up excuses, like, "Yeah, well, he doesn't live where I live," or, "His old man don't beat him upside his head," or whatever. The reason I say this to you is that it is an excuse, a handicap. If I can eliminate with these next few stories some handicaps for you, then I think you can find everything you are looking for.

I have a very good friend by the name of Dick Gregory. Dick is a comedian and a social activist. He went the longest in the world without food, something like 60 days, just to prove a point about a vitamin pill that he was developing for Third World people.

Well, Dick Gregory told me one time that they were sitting at a civil rights meeting in Atlanta, Georgia, and everybody was depressed because they all had a handicap. He said that everybody was talking about their handicaps, about "this damn racist society, we can't do anything."

One of the major issues they were talking about was the busing incidents. There was a thing where the blacks had to ride in the back of the bus and they were all depressed, saying they couldn't change that. And finally Martin Luther King hits the desk, and says, "All you people in here are trying to use a handicap. We are going to close down all the buses in this country until we can ride in the bus properly. If the door to opportunity doesn't open with polite knocks then kick the darn thing open!"

Dick told me, "If we would have left the meeting with the handicap, nothing would have changed." But because Martin Luther King decided to not let any handicap stand in his way to changing things for the better, the situation on the buses changed.

Then I think of a young lady, nine years of age, who was told she would never walk again. She was badly burned and also had a bone disease. That lady, Wilma Rudolph, I watched in the 1960 Olympics win four gold medals for this country.

And then when I feel sorry for myself I also think of a young boy in Nashville, N.C., 11 years old, playing catch with his brother, and the ball goes over his head and across the train tracks. In his excitement to get the ball, he runs to get it and the train hits him and severs the lower part of his body. He was in the hospital for 11 months, and they had to cut off his legs. At 15 years of age, Dicky Bryant won the North Carolina wrestling state championship in the 98-pound division.

And, finally, if you have a handicap I want you to think of this girl named Kay Vandivier, from Devils Lake, North Dakota. Listen to her handicap. She decided she wanted to go to the largest women's bowling tournament in the world, so she went there and in the last game of the evening she bowled a 300. She was ecstatic; she could finally quit her job in North Dakota, she was going to go to the top of the bowling world — big money, television, the whole thing. But she hit a train while in her car at a crossing and got pinned under it. They rushed her to the hospital, and at first they pronounced her dead. She was badly lacerated, and her head was almost cut off from her body. They had to cut off her right arm to keep her living. They called in her parents because she wasn't going to live. Remember, she had just bowled a 300.

Somehow she lived, she hung on to a cord of life. She was in a coma for a full year, never opened her eyes, never put her feet on the ground. Doctors said she would never walk again if she came out of the coma, but five years to the day of her accident, Kay Vandivier bowled again. She entered the North Dakota state tournament, and in the last game of the night she bowled a 295 and became the North Dakota woman's champion. She did it with her left arm, because they had cut her right one off. There's an old saying, "I complained I had no shoes until I saw a man who had no feet." Her 19 ounces, her brain and her heart, she held onto. She told herself that she could, that she wasn't afraid to fail, that she wasn't going to accept her handicap. She decided that she wanted to move to the mansion on top of the hill instead of the trailer at the bottom, living on welfare and taking people's crumbs.

And now, hurdle No. 4. I wish I could tell you I have mastered it, but it is a bitch. It is the one most people take to the grave with them. See, you can run the race and be cool, but it is when you are alone that you really know who you are and what you want out of life. Socrates put up in the biggest of the Greek temples only two words, "Know thyself." Shakespeare wrote throughout his writings, "Be true to thyself." And the Bible says throughout to know yourself. Don't forget this last hurdle; most of us run around this hurdle, we act like it isn't there.

You can get to the top without going over this hurdle. How would you like to be one of these three guys? The president of the largest steel mill, a billionaire. Or a man the *Wall Street Journal* said had the greatest monetary mind. Or a man taking his victory lap with an Olympic gold medal around his neck and 105,000 people standing and cheering for him, chanting "U-S-A." Didn't these men lick the first three hurdles? The "I can't," "afraid to fail," and "handicap" hurdles?

But look what these men did, they forgot the last hurdle. The president of the largest steel mill, a billionaire, died penniless. The man who was the greatest financial mind spent the last few months of his life institutionalized and died in a corner, by himself, in an insane asylum mumbling. The man with the gold medal and the crowd cheering him, six months later he slit his wrist and died on the floor of a cheap London, England hotel.

And finally I leave you with two thoughts. Every October 15th when practice starts, I leave this thought in my players' minds, and it is the closing thought that I want to give you. It is a poem, which you will all get when you leave camp. It is called "Thinking," and it goes like this:

If you think you are beaten, you are,
if you dare not, you don't.
If you'd like to win but think you can't,
it's almost a cinch you won't.
If you think you'll lose, you've lost,
for out in the world we find that success begins with a fellow's will.
It's all in the state of mind;
if you think you are out-classed, you are.
You have got to think high to rise;
you have got to be sure of yourself before you can ever win a prize.
Life's battles don't always go to the stronger or faster man,
but sooner or later the man who wins is the man who thinks he can.

If you can, just leave here with that. Don't let anybody degrade you. All through mankind people have had to do something to somebody. If it wasn't the Jews, it was the Catholics, if it wasn't the Catholics it was the Baptists, if it wasn't the Baptists it was the blacks, if it wasn't the blacks it was the Irish. That's a bunch of bull. That's why man has to stand up for man. Honestly, some of you sitting here today don't really believe in yourself. Oh, you do when you get on the court, but when you leave here, just remember: if you think you can, you can.

Finally, good people must stand up for good. There was this guy preaching hate, racism and so on. They said, "This guy is no good, throw him in jail, that will cool his heels." In jail, the guy writes a book called *Mein Kampf*, meaning "My Struggle." This book outlined exactly what he was going to do, and then they let him out of jail and millions and millions of people lost their lives because of Adolph Hitler.

He was able to kill all those people because guys didn't have the guts to stand up for what was right! They slept at the meeting, or they thought, What can little old me do? They didn't know they were going to burn anybody. If 50 people would have stood in the way of one of those box cars going to one of those terrible concentration camps, maybe they would have been shot down, maybe 5,000 people would have lost their lives, but not 30 million people. And it all goes back to those 19 ounces.

Please leave here believing in yourself. Don't let anybody con you, or jive you. No pill, prayer, or prescription can give this to you — you've got to give it to yourself. You have got a tremendous amount of beauty here; God doesn't make any junk.

And, finally, I want leave you with this. Man can fly faster and higher than any bird in the history of the world. Man can dig faster and deeper than any burrowing creature. The only thing man hasn't learned to do is walk on earth like a man.

Have a great journey.

Bernard King is a patient man. He proved that by coming back from career-threatening injuries twice during his professional career, and he did it again by signing autographs for nearly two hours after his address to Five-Star campers. King played for the New Jersey Nets before retiring after the 1992-93 season, but this lecture was given when he was a member of the New York Knicks in 1988. Many of the following comments came during a question-and-answer session with the campers.

★Bernard King

I'm really happy to be here. Our season is over now. We didn't win the world championship, but we were fortunate to advance to the second round against the Boston Celtics. I think we did a good job taking them to the seventh game, and maybe next year we can win the championship.

During the playoffs I played with two dislocated fingers. The only way I was able to play was with two plastic casts on my middle finger and ring finger and having them taped together. They're still healing, so I can't do anything in clinics as far as shooting yet.

Growing up in Brooklyn, I had many dreams and aspirations and goals. One was to grow up and be like Sidney Poiter. I fell short of that one. Another was to grow up and become part of the Olympic team. Back in 1972 I can remember watching the Olympics on television, and it really did something to me. I think it lit a fire in my belly. I said to myself, One day I'm going to challenge to make the Olympic team.

In 1976, when I was attending the University of Tennessee, I had the opportunity to try out for the Olympic team. I trained like I had never trained before. Unfortunately, I failed in my bid to make the team. That really hurt me. I think that was the first time in my life I cried about anything associated with basketball. It was the only time in my life, in terms of basketball, that I had failed at something instead of succeeding. I realized at that point you have to pick yourself up, dust yourself off and move on.

That's when I began to realize there are obstacles in life. I've encountered a few of my own. There's a number of hurdles you have to clear and a few mountains you have to climb along the way. I've been fortunate in my life in that I've been able to get over those huge mountains.

But I had another dream. I wanted to grow up and play for the New York Knickerbockers one day. I'm proud to say that I am the captain of the Knickerbockers.

My basic point is that a lot of you here have a dream of playing professional basketball. I had the same dream that you have. But I want to tell you, not too many of you are going to make it. I'm just being realistic about it. I wish you luck. I'm here to tell you that dreams can become a reality. They became a reality for me. But I'm also here to tell you that one out of a million athletes make it in the NBA. Become the best athlete that you can be, train as hard as you can, work on the fundamentals, listen to as many people as you can. But don't put all your eggs in one basket, because the chances of it working out aren't that great.

Many of you are going to receive the opportunity of going on to college. I went to the University of Tennessee. I left after my junior year, so I didn't attain my degree. But you have the opportunity to do something with your lives, and the only way you can do that outside

I consider everything in life to be a challenge. That's the way I approach it. That's the only way I can excel at anything I can do. A lot of people said there was no way I could play with a dislocated finger, but I considered that a challenge. I concentrated a little harder on the task at hand, and that was the way I was able to play.

I psych myself up for every ballgame. We play 82 games, plus the playoffs. I think a great many players bail themselves out. They use the long season as a copout for not being able to sustain an emotional level. I don't believe in that. I think every time you step out on the court, whether it's in your hometown or it's in a gym by yourself, you should go out and play the hardest you can, and play with emotion, because that's the way the game should be played. The way I do that, I pretend the team we're playing against is trying to embarrass us, personally trying to embarrass me. I never want to be embarrassed.

I'm a firm believer in training during the off-season. I love long distance running. I run three to five miles every day when I'm training in addition to playing every day.

People wonder how I get in condition to play on back-to-back nights. It goes beyond physical conditioning. You have to condition yourself mentally to play on consecutive nights. I make it a challenge to play better on the second night than the first. I'm proud to say I generally do. Too many players use it as a copout. If you don't think you're tired, you won't be tired.

Despite what some of you may have heard, I've never had a drug problem. I've had a drinking problem; I am an alcoholic. I can't drink. I don't drink. I think that growing up, being an athlete, by the time I came to the NBA, I had to face some harsh realities. One was that you can't just be happy as a professional basketball player. You have to be more than a professional basketball player. That was a problem that I faced. I've been able to overcome that difficulty; it's out of my life. I have to deal with it all the time, but I haven't had any relapses.

Anything that you do during the course of a game as far as making mistakes, you should rectify those mistakes the next day in practice. You're learning constantly. I didn't have an outside shot when I came into the league, I didn't handle the ball very well when I came into the league. My footwork is not as good as it is now when I came into the league. I pride myself on coming back every year a better player than I was the previous year.

When I was growing up, I probably didn't work enough on my jump shot. But basketball is confidence. If you don't have confidence in yourself as a player and person, you won't be successful. If you work hard enough, you'll become a better player, and I work on the things I'm weak on all the time.

People didn't give me things when I was growing up just because I was a basketball player. That's why I work as hard as I do. I like to think of myself as the hardest-working player in the NBA. I don't think of myself as one of the best players in the NBA. Once you start to think of yourself as the best, you don't work as hard and you start to decline. I wasn't given things. Everything I've got today was earned.

I hate losing. Anytime I lose, I hate it. I go home and replay the game in my mind and think about what I could have done to keep from losing. But when you play 80-some games, you're going to lose, and you have to learn to deal with it. The thing to do is give everything you have, and when you know that you gave 100 percent in every game, it's a little easier to deal with.

I've never had an attitude problem as far as getting along with my coaches or teammates, but I had a severe problem dealing with losing, particularly when I was in high school. After a ballgame, you knew you shouldn't talk to Bernard. I've learned to cope with that over the years.

These coaches here are here to teach you guys. Often times in life, whether it's basketball or something else, we close our ears because we think we know everything. When I was your age, I guess I thought I knew everything too. But since I've been in the NBA, my ears are always open. If I can learn something, I learn it quickly, and I try to apply it. I suggest that you do the same thing. If you see another player doing something that you feel you can add to your game, you should take it. As an example, I've borrowed something from Larry Bird. Larry Bird ball-fakes a lot. Have you noticed that? I had never done that until this year. And Moses Malone is the one that I learned the fadeaway jump shot from.

You can always learn from other people. Keep that in mind.

Thank you.

Mike Krzyzewski proved long ago that nice guys don't have to finish last. His Duke program is one of the nation's elite, widely respected for its impressive standards and success. Since 1986, the Blue Devils have advanced to the Final Four six times. They won the national championship in 1991 and '92, becoming the first team to win back-to-back titles since UCLA in the 1970's. Consider Coach K's two other championship game appearances (1986 and '90) and his NCAA Tournament winning percentage — better than 80 percent — and it's obvious his status is unparalleled.

★ Mike Krzyzewski

What I'm going to be working on today is offense, and I'm going to try to give you some things that you can use in shooting and in screening that will help every one of you guys become better players. These are exactly the things that we do daily with our own players at Duke, and I think that they are one of the main reasons that some of those kids develop into such outstanding players.

A lot of you practice shooting. Or at least you think you're practicing, because you go out and throw up some shots. You're out there for about an hour and you come back in and you tell everybody, "Yeah, man, I've been working an hour on my shooting. I put in a lot of time." The thing is, you really haven't put any time in.

Now, that doesn't mean you shouldn't be out here, just screwing around and practicing with the ball, because basketball should be fun. But what you need to do when you're practicing your game is to make things game-like. That's the key to becoming a good basketball player. It doesn't make any difference how long you practice, it's how *well* you practice. I would rather have my players practice for five minutes on shooting, but do it at the right pace, than go out and shoot for 45 minutes at their own pace, because they're wasting time.

Let's do this drill right now. How many of you at times play two-on-two? One-on-one? How many of you have girlfriends? You can do these drills if you have three guys on the playground, two guys and a girlfriend, two guys and a little brother, or two guys and a father who puts his nose too much into what you're doing, maybe.

But the thing I want to get across is that you do things in a game-like situation. What I want you to do right now, I want you to set your defender up. Every time, before you shoot the ball, I want you to set your man up with what I call a V-cut. Take him in one direction, and as he goes back in this direction, I cut back to receive the ball. When I receive the ball my feet are facing the basket, so now, when I go up, the shot goes in because I've prepared myself to shoot the ball.

So many of you only prepare yourselves to catch the ball. You set your man up and your legs are straight, not with your feet facing the basket. That's why so many of you can only make moves off the dribble. We want you to make effective use of the ball as soon as you catch it. So I want you to be able to catch the ball and shoot.

Another important ingredient is to talk. Each one of you will become better players if you learn how to talk on the court. One of the things I believe our team does a great job of is talking to one another. You begin that talk process in a drill process by calling out the man's name who's gonna pass to them. In other words, we have our players set V-cuts, and when they come up they yell, "Scott!" They're calling for the ball. How many of you, when you get open this week and your teammate does not throw you the ball, get frustrated with the guy? Well, call out his name and tell him that you're open before it's too late.

Now, when you yell, what happens with your hands? They go up and out. If I make a cut, you're not going to pass the ball to me if my hands are down, right? A lot of you guys do that. First of all, a lot of you don't even set up your man. You're just out here on the perimeter, and you're like this and you hope they're going to throw you the ball, instead of asking for it with your hands out. By talking, you get your hands in a ready position. And also by talking, can you be thinking about anything else? You can't be. And what's one of the main requirements to being a good shooter? Concentration.

Another thing to remember is the shot fake. I've watched a thousand kids play this summer, and you know how many kids shot fake? Only about one percent. Kids don't shot fake, and the shot fake is one of your best weapons if you want to be a good scorer.

Now, we're going to add another thing to teach fakes. After you have set up your man and caught the ball, you can pass fake. This is another move that just isn't taught. We want a shot fake and we want a pass fake, because we want to screw the defense, right? We want to make 'em think we're doing one thing when actually we're doing another, right? Have you guys ever done that before?

I had that happen to me last week when I was up here for Five-Star, except it wasn't in basketball. It was at one of the local bars that Garf goes to after a bad day of camp. I go over with him and get a Coke. I don't drink, but there's a guy next to me who's a real big drinker. You know how you have pitchers of beer? How many of you guys know that? You're not supposed to know that! This guy's sitting next to me, and it's a real slow night in the bar and he's drinking these pitchers of beer. I mean, one right after another. And you know how it is with beer, when you drink you usually have to go to the bathroom.

So, there's just a few other people in the bar, and the bartender asks me what I do. And I think I'm hot stuff, you know, I've been to three Final Fours. Some people will be impressed. And I said, "I coach Duke in the ACC."

"I'm not a basketball fan," the bartender says, "Who cares about basketball?" So he asked the guy next to me, "Well, what the hell do you do?"

So the guy says, "I don't do much of anything. I make a few bets."

"Bets? What do you mean, bets?"

And the guy says, "Well, I'll bet you 10 bucks that I can lick my right eyeball."

The bartender turns around and he sticks out his tongue. He doesn't have as big a nose as I do. His tongue doesn't even touch his nose. So he says, "This sucker can't, there's no way he can lick his right eye. OK, 10 bucks."

Well, the guy who makes bets takes out his glass eye and goes lick, lick, lick, and licks his right eye. So the bartender is getting a little bit pissed, because he's not getting any tips tonight, there's not many people in there. So he says, "What else do you do?"

"Well, that's all I do."

"Let's make another bet," the bartender says.

"Well OK, I'll bet you I can bite my left eye."

The bartender says, "Well, I know the son of a bucket isn't blind. He doesn't have two glass eyes. OK, another 10 bucks."

Well, the guy that makes bets takes out his false teeth and goes bite, bite, bite. So now he's lost 20 bucks. And the bartender is really pissed now. It's one of these bars where you have swivel seats, and the bartender's in a white apron. So the bartender says, "OK, I gotta get my 20 bucks back. Let's make another bet."

"OK, you take those three glasses off the shelf there and put them right here on the bar. I really have to go to the bathroom right now. I really have to go bad. You come over here, you can swirl me around, I'm gonna unzip my fly, and I'm going to go to the bathroom. I'm going to take a leak, and I'll bet you 20 bucks that everything goes into those three glasses."

Now, I'm a Polish guy, and we're sometimes talked about as not being the smartest people, but, I get away from there. I go behind one of the pillars and I'm watching this with interest.

Well, the guy zips down his fly. The bartender comes around, and I tell you what, he's mad, and he swirls the chair around hard. And the guy's going around, and as he's going around it's going everywhere. It's flying, and it's that disgusting yellow. I mean, it's sickening; it's horrible. The bartender's white apron is now yellow; it's disgusting. It's probably like some of your roommates here at camp, the guys that don't wash their clothes.

Finally, the stool stops, he stops, and there's not one drop in those three glasses. The bartender now is just laughing his ass off. And he says, "I knew you couldn't do it! I knew you couldn't do it! I won 20 bucks! I won 20 bucks!"

All of a sudden, down at the other end of the bar, he hears a slam. And some guy down at the other end of the bar just hits his head and collapses on the bar. The bartender says, "What the hell's wrong with him?" And the guy who makes bets says, "When I came in here I bet him a thousand bucks that by the end of the night I'd be pissing on you, and you'd be laughing about it."

It's the same thing, fellows; that's the way the game of basketball has got to be played. It's gotta be played so that when you're on offense, you can't allow the defense to pee on you. You've got to pee on the defense. And you do that by developing the shot fakes and ball fakes. OK?

Remember, most of the game you are not going to have the basketball. What you want to do is to be able to react effectively when you don't have the ball. Now on our team, Robert Brickey, he's our captain for next year. Robert Brickey will play approximately 32 to 34 minutes a game. Guess how much of that time he will have the basketball? A lot of you are guessing two to three minutes. I think if he has it for more than 45 seconds it will be a long time. He'll probably only have the ball for 30 seconds, so what he does without the ball puts him in a position that when he gets it he can do something with it. You want to make effective use of your time on the court. So don't just practice these things with the ball.

Now we're going to talk about screening. Screening, fellows, is the most effective way of producing scoring opportunities. The guy who knows how to screen can become a hell of a basketball player. During the 1984 Olympics, I had an opportunity to spend six weeks helping out with that Olympic team under Coach Knight. During that time we had guys like Ewing, Tisdale, Perkins, Robinson and Jordan. Jordan, during that time, was one hell of a player. Nobody knew that he was going to become the unbelievable player that he is today, but in our motion offense we wanted Michael Jordan to be the focal point of our motion. Pretty good decision, wasn't it? Doesn't appear to be that hard right now. But with all those great players, I thought Coach Knight did an unbelievable job of identifying it. And he had a rule for Jordan: "You can't take a shot until you make one screen."

And you know what? Every time he made a screen ... I shouldn't say every time, 90 percent of the time when he set the screen, he got open. He was helping another guy to get his shot and because of it, it caused a lot of disruption through the defense and he got his shot. And that created a great motion offense for us. That's what I'd like you guys to be thinking of. Think of yourselves as screeners. In our system last year, a lot of times we would have Ferry screen; screen and then shape up, and most of the time he was open. It's helping another guy out.

I think this is a good time to just talk about helping each other out. When I'm at these all-star camps watching kids play, I believe that a lot of kids just play for themselves. They don't play to help their team-mates out. Now you can be a good player, but I'll tell you what, whether it be a college coach from Division II, Division III, low Division I, or the highest of Division I teams, the thing that we all look for are team players — players who are going to help one another out. We look for players who are gonna screen for each other.

Like if I'm with Will, and Will fumbles my pass and lets it go out of bounds. I've seen throughout the summer so many kids, after they've made that pass and their teammate makes a mistake, go "Oh, man!" Instead of saying, "All right, I'll get you next time, are you OK?" It's helping one another out. And we try to do this as a coaching staff too.

Now this is a true story — it's not about pissing or making bets or anything. This is a true story, and this shows the type of relationship our team has. It's late February, and we're playing Arizona at the Meadowlands. They're the No. 1 team in the country. I think we're ranked fifth or sixth. It's a hell of a basketball game. They go out to a big lead, then we come back. It's a close game. And in the last 10 minutes it's back and forth. And you have the two best players in college basketball last year, Danny Ferry and Sean Elliott going at it.

All of a sudden, it comes down to two points. They're shooting the free throw and they miss. Danny Ferry gets the ball and throws it the length of the court and he hits Christian Laettner. He's fouled before he even takes the shot, so there's a one-and-one with one second left. Arizona calls a timeout to freeze Christian.

Now, as a coach, I'm not sure exactly what you say to a kid in that situation. So I try to feel it out. Does the kid need my support? Does he need me to just be quiet? Christian sits down and says, "I got it, Coach, I got it." I think Christian's gonna be one of the fabulous players in the country during his four years at Duke. He's played a hell of a game, and I believe he's going to hit it. So I go through my defensive assignments.

Christian goes to the line and he shoots the ball. The ball goes long, and it hits the back of the rim. Usually, if you know something's going in, you won't follow your shot. Christian just stood there, stunned, the ball missed, and Sean Elliott got the rebound and the game was over.

Two things happened at that point which give me the chills just to think about. It's one of the things that I'll remember most about coaching, and the thing that I love most about coaching is when these things happen. Danny Ferry is right here, Quinn Snyder is right here. Danny Ferry is in a head-on competition with Sean Elliott for Player-of-the-Year. If he wins the game, there's a chance that more people will vote for him. But Danny's not even thinking about that. Christian misses and Quinn and Danny, the very first thing they do is to go right up to Christian and they say, "Are you OK, Christian? You OK?"

Now, the first thing I do is come off the court. I probably should shake hands right away, but my first thing is the kid. I come right up to him. I look right in his eyes and I say, "Christian, that's all right. Don't worry about it, OK?" We go back to the locker room, and former President Nixon was at the game. He comes into our locker room, and he says some nice things. He tells Christian, "Don't worry about the mistake. I've made a few mistakes myself." It's true. Even though we lost, I had to hold myself from laughing at that point. Christian, being a strong player, let it stay right there. He didn't carry it around.

We're playing a month later in the Meadowlands, in the third round of the NCAAs. We have to play Minnesota, and then we have to beat Georgetown to make it to the Final Four. In the Georgetown game, Laettner ends up having his best game. He has an unbelievable game, 23 points and nine rebounds, and we beat a fantastic Georgetown team. I don't know if we'd beat them again if we played them again, but we beat them on that day.

Now we go to the Final Four, and we lose to Seton Hall. We can't make excuses. We got beat. Seton Hall was better than us on that day. Maybe we would have beaten them on another day. But that day, we got beat.

I get back in the locker room and I start talking. And I'm especially talking to my seniors, because I have three seniors who will never play for me again. Those seniors won 117 games in four years, they averaged 29 wins a season, only seven losses, and besides that, they were great kids. And as I'm talking to them, I start crying. I mean I started crying like uncontrollable. I just started bawling, and Christian was sitting right there, and I'm not sure if he had ever seen me cry, or if he had ever seen an adult cry. I always look to see if the kids are catching what I'm saying, and I saw Christian looking up at me. I don't know if he was afraid, or what. I just couldn't read him right. Finally, I just said. "Listen, you guys, don't put the blame on anybody. You were great. We had a terrific year. Let's just go and eat, and we'll get together again tomorrow morning."

That was at 7 o'clock. At 11 o'clock, I was in my room watching some tape with a couple of my former assistants, when all of a sudden, there's a knock on my door. One of the guys answers the door, and it's Christian. I said, "What do you want, Christian? Why the hell aren't you out doing something?" He doesn't even listen. He says, "Are you OK?" "I'm OK," I say, and he walks toward me and sits down right next to me. I said, "You know, you played a hell of a game." And he did. I said, "You got two or three pretty bad calls, but you played really well."

He's not even listening to me. "You're sure you're all right?" he asks. I say "I'm OK. Now will you get the hell out of here." And he turns around and he starts walking out. He turns around again. "You sure you're all right?"

Well, again, I get chills from it, because sometimes as coaches, we think that our crap doesn't stink or we're the epitome of success. But we're human beings too, and we're part of that team. And for one of my players, especially a freshman, after just playing in the most important game of his life, in the Final Four and losing, for him to have to compassion to come back to my room and check on me is one of the greatest things that has ever happened to me as a coach. I don't have to win a national championship to be successful. I don't have to be No. 1, but I have to have those things happen.

I wonder if you can't take some of those things back to your own team. I wonder at the end of the camp here tomorrow, how many of you will go up to a coach who has been particularly good at coaching you this week, whether it be at a station, a lecture, or your coach during your week at camp. How many of you would say, "Coach, thank you.

Thank you for helping me become better."? When you do that, fellows, you become better, and it'll come back to you. And that's the kind of thing you need to develop an outstanding team. And you're better players because of it, because you're not just thinking about yourself. The teams that have players who only think about themselves, I don't care how talented they are, they're going to get their ass beat. They're not going to get the enjoyment out of playing.

The teams that come together, that care about each other, and approach it that way, they are the teams that win championships. They not only win an ACC championship, or an Eastern Regional championship, by just playing that season, they've won a championship. Because they've gotten a lot out of it.

Another great thing that happened to me ... do you all remember Tommy Amaker? Tommy played for me, started every game for four years for me. He's smaller than any of you guys, he was one of the smallest campers ever. As soon as I saw him play, I loved him. I recruited him for over two years, and he ended up starting every game for four years for me because he knew how to take care of himself.

His freshman year, we're playing in the second round of the NCAA's, in the state of Washington, against Washington when they had Schrempf and Welk, they have a really big team. We're down by two points with nine seconds left in the game. And we have a set where I bring Johnny Dawkins off of one side, Mark Alarie on the other side, and Tommy has a choice of hitting either one for the last shot, or if they miss maybe getting an offensive rebound. Tommy gets to his position and both men are covered, so what should he do? He's gotta shoot the ball, because he's open. He takes the shot, and he misses. They rebound, we foul, and we lose.

We charter a jet for about a hundred people to fly back. We don't get back until about 4:30 a.m. Tommy is sitting in the middle. Alarie is on one side and Bilas is on the other. Tommy looks like a pimple who's about to be squeezed, he's so small in there. The other two guys are sleeping, and Tommy's got his headset on. I walk over to him and I put my hand on his knee. He takes the headset off, and I say, "You OK?" He says, "Yeah, I'm fine, Coach. It was the right shot?" And I say, "Hey, it was the only shot. And you're going to shoot it again and you're going to hit it for us. Don't worry about it."

"I'm not worried about it. I'm fine. By the way, are you going to be in tomorrow morning?"

I said, "Tommy, we're not getting in until 5:00 in the morning. I'll be in a little bit later. Maybe about 10 or 10:30." He says, "Well I'd like to stop in and see you."

So I'm there about 10:30 a.m., and one thing about Amaker, he was always on time. He knocks on my door, and comes in. The very first thing he does is he puts out his hand and says "Coach, I want to thank you for helping me throughout this whole year. It's been a great experience. I can't thank you enough for the way you and your staff coached me this year."

Now, he's already the starter, he doesn't have to butter me up or anything. But that's his first thing. Then he sits down and I say "What do you want? What do you want to talk about, Tommy?" He says, "Coach, how can I get better?"

"Coach, how can I get better?" What an unbelievably simple and yet so unbelievably important statement to make. To ask someone else to help you become better. He recognized the fact that he was good, pretty damn good too, started every game as a freshman in the ACC. I'm not sure that any of you will do that here in this gymnasium. But he wanted to get better.

The thing I'd like to leave you with is, I wonder if you have the courage or the sense to ask that same question of the people who teach you. Do you have the courage and the sense to listen to those people? Not just on the basketball court, but in the classroom. And do you have the courage and the sense to make something of yourself on the court and off the court. All you have to do is ask that simple question to your teachers: "How can I get better?" Then work your ass off doing what they say.

It's been my pleasure to be here. Good luck.

Johnny Newman obviously is a man who doesn't forget where he came from. He has received a key to the city of Danville, Va. (his hometown), established a permanent scholarship in his name at his alma mater, the University of Richmond, and conducts summer clinics in both Danville and Richmond. He hasn't forgotten Five-Star, either. Newman is a veteran of eight NBA seasons so far, with more surely to come. He was traded to the New Jersey Nets early n the 1993-94 season after playing the three previous seasons for the Charlotte Hornets.

★ Johnny Newman

Eleven years ago I was sitting right where you are, and I remember as clear as if it were yesterday I was one of five volunteers to demonstrate for a lecture.

When I was a camper I knew that I could shoot the basketball, but as I learned here at Five-Star, I had to do more that just shoot it. Shooting is very important, and with a solid jumper you can make your driving and passing so much more effective because the defense must honor your jump shot, and that opens up the floor.

I want to give you some ideas and concepts that have helped my shooting. First, when you come on to the floor you should begin by shooting close to the basket, and then work your way out. While shooting near the basket, you should concentrate on your follow-through. The follow-through is, in my opinion, the most important part of the jump shot.

I would like to share a couple of shooting drills with you. First, shoot your jump shot and follow your shot, get the rebound and dribble the ball out and shoot again. If you miss your shot, get the rebound and put it in. A key point in doing this simple warm-up shooting drill is to dribble out quickly and to follow your shot with intensity. This will get you loosened up and provide a more game-like shooting environment.

The next drill, which I did when Rick Pitino was my coach when I played with the Knicks, is done with a partner. You start with one player under the goal with the ball and the other player out on the perimeter getting ready to receive a pass from the player under the goal. The player under the hoop throws a chest pass to the player on the perimeter and sprints out to him trying to block the shot. The player on the perimeter catches the pass and shoots the jumper, attempting to get it off before the partner blocks it. The shooter then follows his shot; if it is a miss he puts it in.

The positions are then reversed — the passer/shot blocker now becomes the shooter and the shooter becomes the passer/shot blocker. This is a great drill that will create a game situation and will allow you to get a lot of shots off in a short amount of time.

If you can shoot the ball and make jumpers, then your drive to the basket is half done because the defense is already up on you and the drive becomes easier. If you are not a good shooter, the defense will play off of you and now it becomes very tough to get to the basket.

Never underestimate the value of a good shot. As the defender commits to taking away your jump shot, you can now go by the defense. Remember that when you drive by the defender you need to drive past him as close as you can get to him. You almost bump him as you drive to the basket. Knowing how to drive past a defender and having a shot fake to go with a good outside shot can make you a serious offensive threat.

There are not very many great shooters today at any level of the game, and that includes the NBA. If you are a great shooter, you have a chance to make it. I am a gym rat. I don't ever need anybody to get me to a gym; I'm self-motivated. During the off-season I wake up at 6 a.m. to go work out by myself. Then I play in fullcourt games in the evenings where I work on the things I practiced earlier that morning.

I am also a big believer in strength training. With dedication to a strength program you can get knocked down and then bounce right back up, and when you drive to the goal and you receive that contact you have the power to get the shot off and have a chance to get to the basket and draw a foul.

Even when I was a college player at Richmond University, the coaches knew that I wanted to be the best player to ever put on a uniform at Richmond. I was always willing to work extra. I tried to be the first to the gym and the last to leave. Anytime I had an opportunity to have a coach teach me something, I jumped at it.

At Richmond I wanted to get my degree as well as improve my game. The ball can be taken away from you, but once you earn your degree, nobody can take that from you. A college education helped me to feel like a whole person, not just an athlete. When my time is up

and I no longer can play basketball in the NBA, I feel confident that I will be able to go on with my life and experience success because I have a quality education to fall back on.

When you choose a school you need to go to a school where they want you and where they want you to earn a degree as well. It is tough to get to the NBA and it is even tougher to stay in the NBA. I never let myself get out of shape. Basketball isn't easy for anybody, but you can use it to get a degree — I did. If you learn to be self-motivated and are willing to learn and do the extra things needed to improve, then you will get a lot out of this game of basketball. Hopefully one of the best things you will get is a college education that nobody can ever take away from you.

At Five-Star camp, they call Dennis Jackson "The Sandman." That's because for years he's been the guy who makes sure the kids get to bed at night. Ironically, he's also the guy who has them on the courts for a pre-breakfast workout each morning. Jackson first came to Five-Star when he was an assistant coach at the Junior College of Albany. He was an assistant at Pennsylvania when it reached the Final Four in 1979, and also has coached at the University of Massachusetts. He's now the Dean of Students at Amherst Regional Junior High School in Massachusetts.

★ Dennis Jackson

This day is a special opportunity because it gives me a chance to speak to you from my heart and render a message that maybe, just maybe, will reach five percent of this audience. Now I know that I am not going to tell you anything that you haven't already heard before or maybe anything you don't already know. But hopefully the message I am going to give to you will be everlasting.

On your camp T-shirt, you have five stars around a basketball. Let's think about what those stars can represent. The first star, gentlemen, symbolizes loyalty. Loyalty is a commitment that you give to someone that is not conditional. A lot of friendships are built on loyalty. This camp is predicated on loyalty. I ask you, who are you loyal to? I hope you are loyal to your family. Your job will be predicated on loyalty. It is the biggest word in the coaching profession. It is the largest word in athletics. Loyalty is everything.

Let me give you an example. How many of you guys are going to fulfill your commitment to this camp as far as the loyalty end of it? Will you be loyal to this camp if you ever make it in the NBA? Will you come back like the great Tyrone "Muggsy" Bogues, who works two sessions and gives something back to the camp? That's loyalty.

My next star deals with the word togetherness. Are you a together guy? There is no "I" in the word team. I had a coach come to me the other day so excited because of how well his team played together. He never said what his record was, he was just excited because they played together, win or lose. I ask you, would you rather score 25 points and lose or score four points and win? Basketball is a team sport, men. There are a lot of guys who have it together. How many of you guys were team players this week? How many of you were sacrificing yourself for the betterment of the team? Because that's what it's all about. It is not about me, it is not about I, but it should always be about us or we.

Now there is a guy in the NBA who made some statements this year — some I agree with and others I do not. His name is Charles Barkley. He said, ``Just because I play basketball I don't necessarily have to be a role model.'' He's right. He said, ``Just because I dunk a basketball doesn't mean I have to raise your kids.'' He is right about that as well. The problem is, if you are going to play basketball you should be part of the team. And with those statements, he is telling me he doesn't want to be part of the team anymore. I would be honored if I could be one of your role models, and you should be honored if you could be someone's role model too.

That's the only problem I have with Charles Barkley — he is forgetting about the kids. See, not everybody has two parents. There are a lot of guys sitting right here who don't have a dad at home. Being a basketball player in this society means you have to be a role model whether you like it or not; that comes with the territory. If you don't want to be a role model, keep it to yourself. I am not being negative on Charles Barkley, because I don't know the man. I just know what I heard. The only thing people will know about you who have never met you is what you say. Don't go around saying things like Barkley did — keep it to yourself. The last camp I spoke to, one-third of the camp was wearing Air Max shoes — Charles Barkley's shoes. So don't say you want to be part of the team on one hand and then on the other say you don't.

Let me tell you, I've seen a lot of things here at Five-Star. It was several years ago, back when we had some real tough dudes. I used to go around and check every room and I went to this one room that still had the light on and I go in and I see a black guy and a white guy breaking a peanut butter and jelly sandwich together. That was one of the greatest things I ever saw. They were a team, with one sandwich. I ask you, will you always be a team player?

My next star deals with the word honesty. Are you honest with your ability? A lot of us think we are better than we really are. That's OK, I like that a little bit. But I ask you, tonight after dinner when Mr. Garfinkel reads that all-star list, will you be dishonest about your ability and start to blame others and say that they didn't give you what you deserve? There are a lot of dishonest people in the world today. I was taught to be honest, and I try to teach that to others. You know what, somebody is always watching, and if you think they aren't you are in trouble. When I walk in stores I know the camera is on me. As basketball players, when you walk in stores the camera is on you. Don't ever think you can get away with taking something that isn't yours. Let me tell you, they are building a lot of prisons out there for guys that try to get away with dishonesty.

I was a junior college coach at Albany Junior College and was also a counselor and taught a class in a prison that was minimum security. Now it is maximum security. I walked past a group about this size and they had the worst look on their faces. They had that look that if the gates would have slid back they would have torn me to pieces, because that's how angry they were. They have a place for dishonest people, and that is why I make a commitment to you guys. Do you know that there are 100,000 guns being taken to school every day? Hey, it is rough out here and that's because there is a lot of dishonesty. People are taking short cuts in life.

Let me tell you, there are no short cuts in life. Don't let anybody lead you to short cuts with drugs, with gambling; don't let it happen to you. The easiest thing in the world to get into is trouble, but it is the most difficult thing to get out of. You have a better chance of becoming a doctor, a lawyer, a computer programmer, than you have of becoming a pro basketball player. You have less than one percent of a chance of becoming a pro basketball player.

My next star deals with the word adversity. Adversity. We all will face adversity in our lifetime. Adversity introduces men or women to themselves. I ask you, do you know who you are? I know who I am and I know where I am going. I want you to know who you are. You talk about adversity, ask Michael Jordan, who sat right here in camp, if he knows what adversity is. Everyone experiences the highs and the lows, the good with the bad, the bitter with the sweet. What are you going to do about it? Will it make you stronger?

I love talking to kids and I love talking to parents. I was talking to the parent of a kid here in camp the other day and after awhile he pulled out a key chain, and on it read ``Tough times never last, but tough people do.'' You gotta be tough when you face adversity, because we don't know how it is going to hit. See, there is adversity waiting for a lot of you in the little book that Mr. Klein and Mr. Garfinkel gave you in the recruiting seminar that tells you what you need for Proposition 16 and 14. All you guys know about now is Proposition 48, but Prop 16 and 14 go into effect in 1995. You heard what you need! Getting a 2.0 GPA and 900 SAT, that's adversity. I don't agree with Prop 16 and 14, especially in inner-city schools where the funding is inappropriate and a variety of other things that make it nearly impossible for kids to get the needed scores. But I am trying to help with my organization — P.L.A.Y., which stands for ``playing, learning, achievement for you.'' It is a non-profit organization that invests $1500 in every individual that wants to come and we tutor you in 33 hours of SAT preparation, reading and writing skills, study skills, note-taking skills, research skills, quantitative skills so that you will not fall short of these guidelines. We all will face adversity, but what will you do? See, here's the thing, we all got to take a fall. When your fall comes, land on your back, because if you can look up you can get up.

My next star deals with the word love. L-O-V-E, gentlemen. It is a very simple word. A lot of people confuse something that is simple with something that is easy. They sound alike, but are different. It is simple to get up here, but it isn't easy. It is the same with this love thing. You got to have a love for the game, but most of all you got to have a love for yourself before you can love anything else. There was a guy who I played ball with in high school who wrote me a letter. I hadn't seen him in years. He was a football player, and now he is a great official. In his letter he said, ``I know we haven't seen each other in years, but I love you like a brother.''

We all should love each other like brothers, because you never know what might happen to your real brothers. In 1970, I was driving down the road with my brother and all of a sudden I heard him gasping for his breath. I pulled over to the side of the road and frantically tried CPR, which I didn't know. Believe me, I know it now. The CPR didn't work and my brother died. He believed in the Creator, he lived life in a way that gave something back. You can imagine the pain I felt in losing my brother.

However, to replace my brother, my Creator gave me my son. My son has been in this camp all week and has played well. He has never given me any trouble. Please stand up, son. I love you!

Now, I want everybody to stand up and hold hands. Repeat after me. ``I will persist until I succeed, regardless of how difficult it may be, regardless of the odds, I will let no one, no thing, or no circumstances stop me. I am intelligent. I am tough. I am strong. I am powerful.'' Now, I would like you to look at the person next to you and say, ``You are great and so am I.''

Thank you.

Will Rey has been contributing to Five-Star for nearly 15 years, offering tips on everything from playing the post position to three-point shooting. He was an assistant coach at Evansville for five seasons before landing the head coaching job at Loyola of Chicago. He's made great strides in rebuilding the program in his five seasons there, as the Ramblers have proven to be a dangerous opponent for any team they face.

★Will Rey

I am here today to give you things that will help you improve as a basketball player. Before I can give you specific drills, you need to ask yourself, "How can I improve?" For a player to get better, he must want to get better. This is especially true with regard to one's weaknesses. A weakness in your fundamentals now will become magnified as you go on to college.

Don't confuse athletic ability with being a basketball player. There is a big difference. There are thousands of great athletes throughout this country, but only a handful of great basketball players. Just because you can run and jump doesn't mean that you'll be able to get your shot off against another athlete. Just because you can run the court doesn't mean you can finish on the break.

Many times the difference between being a great player and an average one is the type of attitude you have. Are you coachable? Can you take criticism and profit from it? It will, for some, come down to attitude that will ultimately cause you to get cut. Flaws in attitude will eliminate players from this game.

Will you be one of those that attitude causes you to get cut? Talk to yourself about your own attitude. Attitude is something you can control, regardless of your athletic ability. It would be terrible to have the athletic ability in the range of Michael Jordan or Dominique Wilkins and not make it because you didn't have the right attitude on or off the court. Make yourself be positive. Make yourself be coachable.

Being around Five-Star Basketball Camp for so long, I have seen some common mistakes that players of great talent make. Many of these mistakes are basic and may seem like minor details, but let me quote Tom Heinsohn to show you the importance of paying attention to details. You may know Heinsohn as an announcer for NBA games on TV, but he used to play for the great Boston Celtics teams in the Bill Russell and Bob Cousy era.

Heinsohn said that Larry Bird is such a great player because he is a master of the half-inch. That is the difference between making and not making a play. That little edge. Against good defensive teams, you are only going to have a split second to get your shot off and you have to be ready when the chance comes.

It comes down to basics regardless of the level of play. I am going to give you six simple drills that will make you and your team better if you spend just a few minutes on them each day.

The first is the sweep, pivot and protect drill. This teaches you to be strong with the ball. You've seen it happen when a team is trying to hold a lead at the end of the game and the offensive man picks up his dribble and loses the ball. This type of situation can be prevented by working with a partner. You start on offense and your partner on defense. The man with the ball cannot dribble, he can only sweep the ball low and pivot while protecting the ball with his body and elbows. The defensive man tries to knock the ball away. He can slap and foul in attempt to get the ball. This is done for one minute, then the offensive and defensive men switch.

The next drill works on a very important dribble, the pull-back dribble. It begins by taking two dribbles up, then two dribbles back. When dribbling back, keep the ball behind the back leg and keep your head up. Continue this drill, taking two dribbles up and two dribbles back for one minute with the right hand only. Then switch to the left hand and do the same thing for one minute. The third minute is done by going up two dribbles with the right hand, back two dribbles with the right hand, then executing a cross-over dribble and taking the ball to the left hand and going up two dribbles, back two dribbles, crossing over to the right hand. Repeat this as many times as possible in one minute. You will be shocked how this simple ballhandling drill will improve ballhandling in a short but intense time period.

It is important to remember that everything in basketball is the conservation of time and space. So every drill should be done at a high intensity and each dribble should cover as much ground as possible.

The next drill is called the reverse-the-ball drill, and is done with three offensive players and three defensive players. With a man at the point and one on each wing with defenders on all three, a pass is made to the wing who made a V-cut to get open. The wing catches the ball and squares to the goal. The point, who just threw the pass, should jam the defender toward the goal and pop back (replacing himself). The ball is reversed back to the point, who tries to make the reversal pass to the other wing, who is timing up his V-cut so as to get open just as the point is ready to throw him the ball. This drill continues for one minute. The defense may try to force the ball one way or the other.

The fourth drill is the turn-the-corner drill. With a ball at about the jump ball circle, the man dribbles full speed to the wing area where a cone is placed about foul line extended to 18 feet. The dribbler goes hard to the cone and pushes off his outside foot and goes in a straight line to the goal where he finishes the layup. The dribbler gets his own rebound and dribbles to the jump ball circle, where he does the same thing except to the other wing, where another cone is placed. This drill is done for one minute. The same drill can be applied with the addition of shooting a pull-up jump shot instead of a layup.

The fifth drill is done using three players — one on offense with the ball and two defenders keeping their hands behind their backs the whole time. The offensive player starts with the ball behind the hash mark and dribbles toward the basket. The defenders are waiting with their hands behind their backs. They try to keep him from getting to the basket, and he tries to go around them for a layup. The goal is to get as many made baskets as possible in one minute. After the offensive player makes a basket, he dribbles back to the hash mark as fast as possible and attacks the defenders again. This drill is excellent for the offensive man to work on his skills of getting to the basket. Also, the defenders get defensive footwork practice.

The last drill I am going to show you is the feed-the-post drill. This requires two offensive and two defensive men. The ball begins above the top of the key (point area) with a defender guarding the ball. The other two players, the offensive and defensive men, start on the block. The point dribbles to the wing area below the foul line extended. As the ball gets to the wing area, the offensive post man either sets up his man high to go low to the ball side block, or he sets up his man low to go high to the ball side block. The man with the ball must get the ball to the post man in a position to score. After the post pass is made, the offensive man tries to execute a post move to score. Techniques like faking a pass high and then passing low are used by the passer.

The object of this drill is to get the offensive man to understand the angles needed to effectively post feed, while the offensive post man learns how to get himself open to receive a post pass and then score.

A common mistake that I have seen this week in camp is in relation to the man with the ball going to the basket. Anytime you break the top of the key you must take your eyes to the rim, lower your dribble and work off the two-foot jump stop. So many guys are losing the ball as they break the key area or they are getting called for a traveling violation as they pick up the ball off the dribble. These turnovers can be prevented by doing the three things I just told you. Focus your eyes on the rim, lower your dribble, work off the two-foot jump stop.

As you work on your game, you need to constantly put pressure on yourself to improve. You do this by using time or by using opponents. What I mean by using time is to do things like attempting to make five shots from the free throw line in 20 seconds, rebounding your own shot and dribbling the ball back out to the foul line area. Simple drills utilizing a clock can help you become more efficient by putting pressure on you to get past your comfort zone, which makes you improve.

Using opponents is an excellent way to improve *if* you can get opponents that are better than you and/or that are willing to work extremely hard and have the desire to improve. With an opponent (workout partner) you can take 15 minutes and really make yourselves better players if you are willing to do some high intensity, fundamental drills.

Don't be afraid to try something new. Many of you fear embarrassment and in turn you won't practice something a coach has shown you. Listen to the coaches here and go out and work on the things you have learned. Forget about those that may try to make fun of you for trying a new move and screwing it up or for doing one of the drills I have just shown you. In the end, you will be the one who will make the team while the ones with the bad attitude or the fear of trying will be the ones who get cut.

Good luck, gentlemen, I hope you learn to master the half-inch and the basics.

Every basketball fan knows Dick Vitale, the commentator who seems to pop up with a microphone at every big game. Not everyone knows that this man of boundless energy was a successful coach in an earlier life. After coaching high school ball in his native New Jersey, he became an assistant at Rutgers, helping the Redmen to the Final Four. He then took over at the University of Detroit, and is the only coach in the school's history to get a team into the NCAA tournament. He then coached the NBA Detroit Pistons. He gave this lecture in 1988, a year after surviving a horrible auto accident.

★ Dick Vitale

I'm not gonna be here today to joke with you. I tell a lot of stories and I have a lot of fun with basketball; I love basketball. But I love people and I love youngsters more, and I love what the game has done for me.

See, you're all chasing a dream. Every one of you here today, I'll guarantee you when you go to bed at night, you dream it. You say, wow, maybe, maybe if I put the Five-Star shirt on, all those people will analyze my talent and write about me, and maybe I'll get all kinds of collegiate offers. Now I'm that boy; I got my ball, and I got my dreams.

See what bothers me so much is too many of you, in chasing that dream, forget about all the basics in terms of becoming not just a basketball junkie, but a person who can make it in the biggest game of all, the game of life. And you say, "Why are you saying that, Dick?" Well I'm gonna refresh you.

It hurts when I pick up the paper and I read about some former great athlete, who maybe I had the opportunity to be on television with, to evaluate his game, and I read about him entering a drug rehabilitation center, or read about him entering an alcohol rehabilitation center, because of those two magical words that he couldn't deal with, and that many of you have a tough time dealing with: peer pressure. "My peers, baby, they mean it all." They mean bull. They mean zero. It's you as a person. It's you as an individual.

I'd give anything in my life to have my mom be living today, because I came that close, that close to going off the deep end. But, man, I was like on cloud nine when I went to the Meadowlands a couple of months ago and I heard these voices crying out from the stands: "Hey Richie, hey Richie, remember us!" I looked up and saw some guys I went to school with, 20-some years ago, in East Rutherford. I coached at East Rutherford High. I went to high school there, and I heard these voices and I waved and I asked them to come on down. And they came down and said to their sons, "Hey, we went to school with him. Tell our sons, didn't we go to school with you. Will you sign some autographs for us?"

I said, "What are you guys doing now, man, what are you doing with your lives?" Now there's nothing wrong with driving a cab, there's nothing wrong with driving a truck, but there's something wrong when you're bouncing from job to job and you have no accountability and you can't deal with responsibility and you can't deal with punctuality. They said, "We're bouncing, man, we're bouncing."

I shook my head and I walked away, and I said, "Thank you, momma, thank you up there in the sky in heaven." My mother, you see, had a fifth grade education, and my father had a sixth grade education. I would come home and she would say, in an Italian sort of way, "What are you doing with your life? You're going nowhere." I'd say, "Momma, don't worry about it." But one day I needed to listen to momma, because my dream came to an end.

I used to go to the playground and play ball. Back in my era, it was a guy that wore No. 14. He played with the Celtics. His name was Cousy. I told Magic Johnson once, I said, "Magic, you were only a gleam in your momma's eye, baby, when the Cooz was going between the legs, around the back, kicking it right, left, playing with the Celtics, a Hall of Famer, baby!" Well, you see, I'd go to the playground, and I'd dream like you. You wear the Five-Star shirt and get the brochure and you look at pictures of Michael Jordan, Isiah Thomas and Dominique Wilkins, and the list goes on and on. I had my dreams too, and I wanted to be Cooz, but I lost the eyesight in my left eye. I was sitting in the doctor's office and he said, "Stop crying, son. Stop crying. You might be blind, but you won't be the only blind person in the world. There are a lot of people who have it worse off than you, so learn to live with it.

I begged and I pleaded and I prayed to be able to play basketball again, but my mother said, "Hey, you've got enthusiasm, why don't you do something with your life?" So I got involved with kids, and got to school, and I got my degree, and I lived in a three-room apartment back in the '70's, and now I cool down in my house that I have, and I tell my wife, who came from New York, her dad was an elevator operator, we pull in front of our house, and we look, and I say, "Hon, look where we live!" I say this not to brag, I say it because I'm proud. We pull in front of my house, and I look at five bedrooms. Five baths. A tennis court. A swimming pool. A three-car garage. New cars.

And you know why? Because of a round basketball, baby. Because I've wheeled it, dealed it and used it. I didn't let the ball use me. And what happens to many of you, you let the ball eat you alive. It consumes your every part of your life. And you forget about all the things that it takes to make it in the biggest game of all, the game

of life. People say, "Well, coach, what are the things that help to make it in the greatest game, the game of life?"

When I go see Magic, like yesterday, I walk in and look at Earvin Magic Johnson and he says, "Hi coach, how ya doing?!" He has a smile on his face and he looks you in the eye like a man, not trying to be Mister Cool. I don't mean to hurt anybody, but I see some cats, man, come strutting in here, and they come like it's lunch time, it's Cool City, USA, the whole bad strut, they come bopping in and they think that shit is so cool, but that gets you to Zero Land. When you're 30 and you can't stick the "J" anymore, and the Vitales and all the other analysts don't talk about you anymore, and now you go for a job, and the guy says, "What are you going to do for me today? What are you going to do here to help us?" You better have learned how to look people in the eye, how to learn, how to shake a hand like a man.

That's all part of growing up. Like learning how to be punctual. A man calls a practice session at 2 o'clock, get there at 1:45, get there on what I call Vince Lombardi Time. Get there early to show them that you're something special. I talked to all the All-American players recently and when I spoke to them, I talked about expectations. I talked about blending. I talked about academic adjustment. And I talked about media. They came here at this camp and you should have seen it, they came up to me after and it was great to get the response, to get the handshake, to look Alonzo Mourning in the eye. I introduced him to Red Auerbach and Red started telling a story about Bill Russell, and when Alonzo walked away Red said, "You know what, I don't know if the kid's a great player, Dick, but boy, he looked me right in the eye when I spoke to him."

Now you say to me, "What do you mean about expectations?" Well, let's say now your dream is realized. Let's say all the recruiters think you're something special. They think you're Mister Big, and they think you can play, and now it's time to go to college. When you walk into the classroom, baby, like when Alonzo Mourning walked into the classroom at Georgetown, they don't expect 10 points, they don't expect three rebounds, they don't expect 15 and 12.

It's just like an Isiah, and a Magic, there's something they possess, baby. You saw it the other day, Magic cracked Isiah when he went down that lane. They love one another, but now they're playing for something you can't buy, and that's the championship ring. You can't walk in and say, "I want to be a champ, Mr. Jordan, could you make up a ring for me so I can proudly wave it?" You gotta earn that sucker. Just like you gotta earn your reputation.

So expectations, how do you deal with that? See what happens? A lot of kids can't deal with it. A lot of kids don't deal with the expectations, because when they go to college, all of a sudden they strut in and they walk on that college campus and 15 other players look at Mr. Big, like you're gonna be, and they say, "So what? We were All-Americans too." And you know what happens many a time? The great player like you, you were option No. 1, now you have to be option No. 4. And a lot of guys can't deal with being No. 4. So you know what they do? They become pouters and sulkers, moaners and groaners, and then they pick up the phone and call the coach back in high school and say, "Hey coach, the head coach doesn't like me, and he doesn't think I can play, it's time for me to go elsewhere, and become a tramp athlete, and to quit when the going gets tough."

Yeah, that happens a lot. People do that instead of looking fear in the eye and saying, "You know what, I'm gonna meet this challenge. I'm gonna do it all the right way." It's the same as I was telling Alonzo and Billy Owens and Laphonso Ellis. I said, "You've all got a little problem. When you walk in the classroom in college, every student there knows who you are. They know everything about you. If you don't care about your reputation, if you don't care about what they think of you as a person, about your punctuality, you've got people across the campus saying you're a dumb jock, an absolute, flat-out zero who doesn't make it in life." So as I told the great ones, go one step beyond. You should worry about your reputation because you live off that, baby. That's your life line, your blood line. You get there early. You show those students that you are special.

You've heard it before, an All-American is an ordinary person with an extraordinary desire to excel. Like Magic, God I could tell you stories about Magic. Six in the morning. Ice, snow on the playground. A young kid dreaming. See, it's nice to dream, but to catch that dream is something special, and the Magic Johnsons of the world shovel the snow, shoot the jumper, handle the rock. A lot of people here are quicker than Magic, quicker than Isiah. Maybe not quicker than Isiah, but they jump higher. Or Larry Bird. Take a look at Larry Bird. You can beat him in a foot race, but do you have all the intangibles? I remember doing a Celtics game, you go there at 5 o'clock and who is running the stairs? The other players aren't there yet. Game time is 8 o'clock. It's April. Here's Larry Bird. He's running the steps, and the sweat is pouring down. You think, Why Larry? You're making $2 mil a year, $3 mil a year! That doesn't matter, because it's that magical word called pride. You saw it the other night with Magic and Isiah, when Magic says, "I'll tell Isiah again, baby, he comes down that sucker lane, he better be ready to pay for it, 'cause I got pride. I wanna win."

It's like with Garf, my man Howard, whom I love. I'm here not because of money, I'm here because of this man, and that gets me to another part of development as a person. It's called loyalties. It's called caring for people. He took me when I was down. I had no job. I was going nowhere in life. I had just finished coaching high school and he heard me speak at a banquet. And he told me I should be coaching in college. I thought I had reached the end. But all of a sudden the phone rang. Again, you never know who you might be impressing. I didn't know Howard. Then the phone rang, and the guy says, "I want to hire you. I want you to be our assistant coach at Rutgers. Come down for an interview. We're gonna really look at you because of Howard Garfinkel." I said, "Really? Really? That man really sold me that much?" And I got the job. I reached my dream. I got that job. And all the doors opened.

See, I don't believe in the word can't, just like you shouldn't believe it. Don't believe you can't be successful. Think positively about whatever you attempt. I disagree with the late, great Vince Lombardi, whom I love. He came from my county, and as a kid I used to go up to Vince Lombardi's school in St. Cecilia, I lived maybe 30 miles away, and I would run up and down the steps and go in the halls and think, Wow, Coach Lombardi of Super Bowl fame used to coach here. Coach Lombardi didn't get his first chance to be a coach on a big-time level as a head coach until he was in his 40's. Then when he got it, all the great things he did in high school at St. Cecilia, they just carried him to the top. Lombardi said that winning isn't everything, it's the only thing. Well, I disagree with that philosophy fellas, and I want you to listen to me. I want to you to listen clearly. Winning to me is the ability of an individual in pursuit of any goal or dream, to give your best.

If you give your best, and you don't play a con game ... see, you can con momma, you can con poppa, you can con the coach, you can con anybody in this room, but you know who you can't con? You can't con you. When you look in the mirror each day, you know the game you're playing. It's nice to be on top of the mountain, it's nice to be recognized as one of the giants, but let me knock you down a peg. Think about 1987. Ready for this? Look at the NBA's first-round draft choices. Twenty-three selections, that's where all the money is. You know how many of those 23 were McDonald's High School All-Americans? You ready for this? Four out of 23. That's right, four out of 23. Kenny Smith, North Carolina fame. Joe Wolf, North Carolina fame. Reggie Williams, Georgetown fame. Dallas Comegys, DePaul. Now let's take a look at the top selections and where they were in high school. The No. 1 choice was a guy nobody wanted when he came out of high school, but he went to the Naval Academy and dedicated himself. He epitomizes what a student-athlete is all about, and I use the word student first. He epitomizes what I believe in, a sense of pride. A lot of guys said, "David isn't ready for the Olympic trials. David would struggle to make the team. David went on a kick. He went on a kick at the Naval Academy because his pride was tested, he got himself in great shape, and he dominated.

That's right, the first pick of the NBA draft was David Robinson. You know what he was in high school? He was wrestler, and he was a football player. But then he fell in love with basketball and then he grew, and while all the other guys that were high school All-Americans thought they were cool, when they were resting on their laurels, guys like David Robinson had the four D's: desire, dedication, determination and a discipline of body and mind. It takes discipline to be special. To be a zip or zero in life takes nothing. Anybody can walk in late. Anybody can run his mouth when he's supposed to be quiet. Anybody can be a loser. But be a winner, baby, be a winner. There are only a handful, and I'm not just talking about being a great athlete.

Then we look at the 1986 draft, and that bothers me more than ever. Do you know that four out of the top seven picks in 1986, they thought they were on top of the mountain too, but they were involved in drugs, and oh, does that hurt. Howard and I ran a basketball game for a boy that lost his two legs and his arm, a kid named Sammy Davis who got hurt in a train accident. Willis Reed and all the great pros came down. When I visit a hospital and I walk through a children's ward, do you know how many kids would give anything to be here like you, to have two legs, two arms, to have a mind that can function?

See, too many of us take all this for granted, we take it all for granted. When you look at the '86 draft and look at William Bedford, here's a guy who's been in drug rehabilitation. I don't say this to tell you a story. I tell you a fact. And then there's Roy Tarpley, he used to be the best sixth man in basketball, but he's been in rehabilitation. And then we look at a guy that's been in trouble all his life, and he's a beautiful kid if you talk to him one-on-one, but oh, he's weak, he's weak. Today he should be one of the giants. You have all these guys who really can't play making millions of dollars, and this guy never did make it when he should have been an all-NBA'er, and his name is Chris Washburn.

Then we go to No. 4. Boy, it tears me apart to go to No. 4, because I thought we were looking at the coming of another great one. Oh, man, he was special. I caught his act on ESPN I don't know how many times, and oh, what a beautiful kid when you rapped one-on-one with him, and today, instead of being in the NBA with the greatest B&B act in all of basketball, that's right, the Bird and Bias Show, he's dead. You see, Bias got weak, 'cause he got cool and he got the cash and he couldn't deal with it. Lenny Bias is a memory. He's history. But you see, we all believe it can't happen to us.

Howard hurt me when he introduced me today, when he said I was tired and might not be 100 percent. Yeah, I'm tired. My game the other night didn't end until 12, then I have a 5 a.m. wake-up call. I got to the airport, had a 7 a.m. flight, then I'm sitting on a plane and the plane is cancelled, then I have to change planes, rush to get here, the whole bit. But you know what, the first commandment of athletics, and the first commandment of life, is when you take on a task, you give it your best. I will never allow anybody to malign my reputation. They may say they disagree with me, and I say, so be it. This is America. But there is no one in this room who could look in the mirror and say Dick Vitale only gave us 50 percent tonight because Dick Vitale was tired.

I don't buy that cry when I hear a player, or I hear a coach, after the game with their favorite cry: "We played with no intensity." Played with no intensity? You played with no emotion? When you lace them up, baby, you have X days; remember this, you have X days in your life to shoot that jumper, and when you lace them up, take advantage of each one of those days. You better make sure at that time you are giving it your best shot to reach your dream. You never know, you might catch that dream.

And please, I beg you, develop within yourself that sense of pride, the ability to persevere when adversity sets in. See, many of you, you're gonna face some adversity. Things are gonna happen in your life that weren't planned, and how do you handle it? Do you quit? You've heard the sayings, about how an All-American is an ordinary person with extraordinary desire, how a quitter never wins and a winner never quits. You've heard about when the going gets tough, the tough get going. You've heard about genius being one percent inspiration and 99 percent perspiration. Any of the giants, whether it be in sports or the corporate world, politics, law, medicine, whatever, they have that tremendous sense of pride and perseverance.

Hell, if I can make it in anything, you've all got a great shot. But I used, all my life, the ability to survive and persevere, to fight and to scrap when the odds were against me. I'll never forget when I started recruiting, and they said, "Dick Vitale, you're crazy to go to Five-Star Camp and think you can recruit Phil Sellers." I recruited Mike Dabney, too, they ended up playing for us at Rutgers, and we went to the Final Four, but I was willing to pay the price, the hours, the letters, the phone calls, the rejections, the hurt, and all the little things that happened. You're gonna face that in your life. You're gonna have a lot of hurts along the way, and how you handle the hurts determines how you develop as a person. Why does a guy get off into the drug scene, the whole bit? Because one, the expectations are so great, so now he doesn't live up to them, and then comes that coach Mr. Leech, baby, oh man, that coach, he don't care for you. He's saying, "You'd be starting for me, you'd be playing for me if I were your coach, you should go somewhere else, you should do this." They start breaking you down.

And then there's R, for respect. If you don't respect yourself, how are others going to respect you as a human being? Why not be the leader? You should have heard Magic last night. My respect for the Magic man went from up here to even higher after the game. That's right. If he were a loser, if he were a pouter, and if he were a sulker, you know he could make all the headlines out there, fellas. But the Pistons have nine players and the Lakers are playing with two. Magic could have walked off the court after being humiliated in his home state in two consecutive games, he could've walked to the end of the bench, he could sat there and put the towel on his face, and he could have pouted, sulked, and the whole bit, but you know what Earvin Magic Johnson did? He went over and put his arm around Kareem, he put his arm around James Worthy, he went over to Michael Cooper, who's three-for-30 or something, and he said, "Don't worry, baby, they're coming home, they're coming to our place."

Yeah, that's a winner. That's not a loser, bitching and moaning about your teammates, your coaches — that means you have no respect. I say respect all, fear none. If Bobby Hurley's supposed to be the best point guard here, you say, "I'm a point guard, I want Bob Hurley, I want to check him. I respect him, but I don't fear him; I want that challenge."

And then we talk about D. Self-explanatory. All the great ones have it. It's called desire. I went into the Chicago Cubs' clubhouse recently, and I'm watching this intense guy. Everybody else is screwing around, they're listening to music, they're playing cards, but there's this one guy in the corner. I even got afraid to go up to him, and I've been around athletes all my life. I watched him in the corner with his bat, he's working on his bat and his grip, and he's like, shaping it, which is legal to do, so you get more bat action, more whip action, and I looked at the intensity of the swings. It's like two-and-a-half hours before game time. He's an MVP, fellas. He makes over $2 million a year. His name is Andre. Andre Dawson. But that's a winner.

You ever see Michael Jordan practice? It's an unbelievable sight. He'll smack you in the face if you're not playing hard. He'll smack you in the face. There's a story they tell over in Indiana. You ready for this one? His name was Larry Bird, and it's the summer, its 95 degrees, and all the rookies of the Pacers are in Market Square Arena working out, and up on top running around the stadium steps is Larry Bird, and the rookies are looking up, they say, "Wow, there's Larry Bird, look at him up there, sweating." One of the guys from the Pacers' office calls him down and asks him if he wants to play with the guys, the rookies. They play five-on-five, in 95-degree weather, a meaningless game. A couple of rooks are fooling around and Larry Bird says, "Hey, man, we're gonna play or I'm leaving. We gonna play some hoops?"

That's why they're winners. Everything they do, they do with a sense of pride, they have the desire, and they culminate it. Like Isiah and Magic, you watch them if their teams win the championship. These are guys that have it all, baby, they have the Mercedes, the Rolls. I've seen Magic's house, it's unbelievable. You pull into Beverly Hills, that's right, a kid from Lansing, Michigan, who didn't have zilch, but he took the ball and he used it. He had no speed, no jumping ability, now you pull into his house at the end of the cul-de-sac, there's a gymnasium indoors, a swimming pool, a Rolls Royce, a Mercedes. He worked harder than hell for all of it. But despite having all that, when he wins, or if Isiah wins, I'll guarantee a bet on it today, you watch these young men, they will be jumping with joy, they'll be kissing and hugging and dancing, and pouring out enthusiasm, because of that game of basketball. It's not about money right now, baby.

These guys are multi- multi-millionaires. But they have those special intangibles. And if you take that word, pride, and you take it into the real world, I say to you, God bless you. You should be commended. You kids are participating for a common goal, to want to be the best you possibly can be. But when it's all said and done, no matter if it's a high school coach, a college coach, a pro coach, somewhere in your life, somebody will call you into the office, whether you're a Kareem or whether you're an Isiah, they'll say it's all over, it is time to go to the stands and be a spectator. If you've applied the principles that got you to the top of the mountain, you are a can't-miss, an absolute can't-miss in the real world. And that's what I love. I love to shake the hand of a Dave Bing, who means nothing to you, but today is a president of one of the largest steel companies and to see the success he's had as a human being, away from the basketball arena, and to watch a Bob Lanier, who I coached, go on into business greatness out in Milwaukee. And you'll see it with Michael, and you'll see it with Earvin, and you'll see it with Isiah, and you will see it with certain guys. And others, they'll be history.

Don't be a guy who, when you hang it up, you can't make it in life. You see, I look at my life guys, and it's all because of basketball. I have guys take shots at me now that you can't believe. The bigger you get, the more visibility, the more exposure, the more you're apt to take shots from people. It's the same way as an athlete, see. Some can handle it, some can't; they pout, they sulk, and they become losers and whiners and cryers.

You see, that ball has been good to me. That ball has been special. It's brought me many a moment of happiness. It's brought me many a moment of jubilation. I've had the thrill of coaching and winning several state championships because I had some great kids. There isn't a coach in America that would tell you that it doesn't start by having some personnel. I was lucky, no doubt about it, and I had the thrill of coaching in high school, college and the NBA.

In 1972, fellas, I was a sixth grade teacher. I go to the teacher's room and I write letters, just like you should do. I try to get in contact with the right people, try to talk to coaches, try to reach out and ask how I can be better, what I can do to improve. I'd write letters to people like John Wooden, who won all those championships at UCLA. Then I'd go into the teacher's lounge, and you know what? This other teacher, Mel, walked in and said, "Dick, what are you doing? You're gonna be a sixth grade teacher all your life. You're not gonna make it."

There's nothing wrong with being a sixth grade teacher. There were great moments in my life then; I love the young kids. But I'd want to be the best sixth grade teacher, so I'd write to John Wooden and I'd say, "Coach, share with me your reasons for success and how you put all those egos together and getting all those great players to blend." And I'd get back a letter that explained the Pyramid of Success and teamwork and mental toughness. When you have those ingredients, you win. I used to tell Mel, "I want to be the best."

You know what happened fellas? In 1978, not too long after I was a sixth grade teacher, I go to Madison Square Garden and I'm coaching the Pistons. All my high school kids, all the kids I coached, everybody that was part of my life, my mother, my father, they're all gonna be there. I'd tell the cop at the door, "Please, this is not the CYO, this is the NBA, tell my relatives I will share a moment with all of them after the game, but I can't now." And then I heard this voice: "Hey Dick!" I turned and I looked, and it's Mel.

He said "Dick, I got my son and my nephew here, come on now, can you give an autograph?" I say sure; now I'm all big-timing, man. I said, "Better than that, come in the locker room. I'm gonna introduce you to all the guys, Lanier, Carr; we'll give you a basketball. We did, and we walked out with my arm around Mel, and I said, "Mel, remember the sixth grade? Remember that teacher's room Mel, when I was sweating and I was writing letters, and I was begging for information, and I was pleading, 'cause I wanted to climb the ladder, Mel, a boy who had a dream, Mel? And remember what you said to me, Mel, that I'm gonna be a sixth grade teacher all my life, Mel? Mel, there's nothing wrong with being a sixth grade teacher, but you know where we are tonight, Mel? Tonight we're at Madison Square Garden, and you know what, Mel? I'm not sitting in the third deck, Mel, I'm sitting at courtside, and I'm the head coach, Mel, of the Pistons, and do you know what that feeling is like?"

Do you know what the thrill is like, to take your dreams, to take your goals, to make them happen? You could do that with your life. First of all, it starts with learning to be a good person. When this camp is over, I'm a failure if you don't go to your respective coaches and you don't stick a hand out, and say, I want to thank you, sir. I paid to come here, but I had the best experience of my life, the first love of my life, sir. I came from suburbia, and it's the first time in my life I sweated with a black kid from the inner city, or a black kid who all his life has seen nothing but black has hugged a white kid, and together, the camaraderie, the togetherness. We're people, man, we are people. We can't change the color of our skin, but we can change our work ethic. That's why I love athletics.

You see it at gymnasiums all the time, you see a white guy like Laimbeer hugging a black guy like Isiah. They don't look and say, "Well, I'm from the rich suburbs of California, my name is Bill Laimbeer, and I was a millionaire as a youngster because my dad made a lot of cash, and you're from the south side of Chicago." You see, that's the beauty of the sport you play, the together sport, the team sport, the sport the greatest athletes in the world play: basketball!

I heard a man speak one time, and he brought goosebumps to my body. I was at a presidential banquet and they're gonna put this gold medallion around this man, and there were thousands, and it was jammed to capacity, and Chris Schenkel was the host from ABC, and I was in the audience, and I had my black tie on, and I watched as all the giants from Ford Motor Company, from Chrysler, from right down the list, General Motors, to Michigan Bell, to the president of the university, and there was this black guy named Jackie James, and he had a Four-Star General's uniform on, and they called Chappie up to the podium, and they said, "Chappie, tonight we bestow upon you the highest honor that the university can bestow, the presidential gold medallion," and Chappie came walking up as proud as can be, and he accepted that gold medallion, and they draped it around his neck, and he turned to the standing room only crowd and looked at the American flag and said, "I only wish my momma could be here today, because momma taught me one philosophy of life. She said, 'Son, extend a hand to all, whether they be black or white, whether they be tall or short, extend it with love, son, and love will come your way.' " And he looked at the American flag and he said, "I've fought many a mission, I've seen bodies die, I've seen people at my feet begging, begging for help," and I began to shake. He was the greatest speaker that I've ever heard in my life.

We lost Chappie several years ago as he was getting ready to give the commencement exercise at the Air Force Academy, the graduation speech. He was special, he touched my life dearly, because he was a winner. He was a winner at life, and he was just like you, and he had dreams. God, I beg you, our paths may never come together again, but I beg you, no matter how tough the situation is at home,

know there are people that will help you. There are people that care. There are people that give a damn.

It all comes down to reality. Last summer at this time I was taught the reality. I came home from California, where my daughters were playing in a national tennis tournament, and I couldn't believe it. I opened up all my mail that was stacked there, and there was one offer after another. Thousands of dollars, six figures, to speak, when I used to get $50. It used to be, "Give me $50 and a sandwich and I'll come." Now I'm doing the same thing, 20 or 30 minutes, for $6,500, $7,500. Are you kidding me? I had all these offers stacked up.

And I had another offer, it's coming out Nov. 1, I'm in a movie! I can't believe it. I'm in a movie with Leslie Nielsen, Priscilla Presley, Ricardo Montalban, all these giants. I went to Hollywood. I couldn't believe it. Played my own role, in a comedy. Yeah, I'm gonna be on that big screen, man, shaking like you can't believe, and oh, I had a ball, and no, Garf, I didn't mention your damn name, so don't worry about it.

And there was this book offer, a whole book of my life, man. I just read the final proof; I can't wait. I hope you get it, I really do, not only cause I'd make a few dollars, but I have a lot of fun in it. I talk about Five-Star in it, I talk about my experiences with coaches and people. Offer after offer is coming in, do this, do that. Just the other day a guy comes up and says he wants to send me and my wife and kids on a cruise with Jimmy Valvano, one week, all expenses paid, and wants me to host a national radio show. I can't believe it. All these things are happening.

So I grabbed my wife, man I love her dearly, 18 of the greatest years of my life, and I said, "Hon, let's go out and celebrate." Well, we went out to celebrate, and we had dinner, my daughters and my wife, and then we came back home, and it was like about three, four minutes from my house when here came a car, riding on the wrong side of the road, a Bronco with the high, high wheels, flying out of control, and my wife was driving, and she couldn't get out of the way. It was the scariest moment of my life. I still can see the lights. I can still see that sucker hitting us head-on. He hit us head on and I hit my face against the windshield, even though I had a seatbelt on. My wife's face splattered against the steering wheel, blood gushing all out, I turned to the left to push my daughters down, and fortunately they didn't get a bruise, but I broke my nose and I broke my foot, I broke my ribs, I shattered a nerve that we have here called the sensory nerve, but most of all, I shattered my right eye socket completely, and that's my only good eye. I'm already blind in my left eye, and I couldn't see for that moment, and I panicked, and I cried and I cried, and I went to the emergency room, and I begged, and I pleaded that that eye would come back, and it started to come back, it was blurry, but I started to see.

But then for the next few days I would go to the rehabilitation ward, and I'd go downstairs, and I'd see people younger than me taking their first step after a major accident, after a major heart attack, after a major stroke, and all the therapists and all the nurses clap their hands like it was the greatest achievement in the world. And when I left there, man, I came to my room, and I was flooded with messages, flowers, phone calls, from almost every school. Howard Garfinkel, he got through somehow, and if you don't think that hit home with me . . . but to see those people, and when I left there, I thought, Screw all the money, screw all that other nonsense, the greatest gift to have is the gift of good health. If we have that, we got a prayer, we got a chance.

I want to say to you, you are lucky people here today. You are lucky to have an opportunity to compete against the best, to participate, to learn all the traits that make a great one. I hope and pray that you take that basketball, you wheel it, you deal it, you use it, you get a sense of pride, perseverance, respect, intelligence, desire and enthusiasm, and then you have the tremendous drive to wanna be the best you can be, but most of all, knowing that if I'm not the greatest player in the world, so be it, but there's nothing to control my effort, and nothing can control my honest approach of making it in the biggest game of all, the game of life — because that's the game we all play.

Don't let peer pressure, don't let the losers of your school, bring you down to their level. Don't you go to that level, to be Mister Cool. As a student, please give it your best. Do you know how many kids today are not going to play college basketball because they don't spend any time in the library? It's too late when you're a senior, man. Jump on that sucker as early as you can. Jump on it every day so you're ready to meet that challenge head on.

You make your decision fellas; I've made mine. I'm coming to the end of my life. I'm 48 now, but man, I wouldn't trade my life for nothing. It has been an unbelievable trip, and I couldn't stick the J. If they gave me the rock, baby, it was absolutely brick city, USA. I couldn't shoot for shit, I couldn't run, I couldn't jump, so I got to where I got by working hard, by busting my guts, and giving my best. And I say to you, Mr. Garfinkel, I love you dearly, you've given me a great opportunity in life, and I'll always remember you for it, but I'll tell you to your face, you know me better than to ever get on a microphone and say that I might give it 50 percent, cause I'll kick your ass like something else. You don't really know Dick Vitale.

God bless you, thank you and goodnight.

Get into the game!

Masters Press has a complete lineup of books
on basketball and other sports to help coaches
and participants alike "master their game."
All of our books are available at better bookstores
or by calling Masters Press at 1-800-722-2677,
or 317-298-5706. Catalogs available upon request.

Our basketball books include the following:

Conditioning for Basketball

By Matt Brzycki and Shaun Brown

Shaun Brown, the strength coach at the University of Kentucky, and
Matt Brzycki, the strength coach at Princeton University, draw from
nearly 20 years of experience in strength training and conditioning in
this book on strength training principles, program design, general and
specific conditioning, conditioning drills, nutrition and flexibility. Includes a conditioning program for the entire year, including the off-
season. Foreword by Kentucky basketball coach Rick Pitino.

$12.95 • paper • 160 pages • b/w photos

ISBN: 0-940279-56-8

Basketball Inbound Attack

By Tom Reiter

The only book of its kind! A comprehensive and effective collection
of inbound plays that can be utilized by teams at all levels. These
proven scoring opportunities feature everything from quick inside
baskets to three-point shots, from every possible formation. Plays for
sidecourt inbound possessions and for last-second situations also are
included. Compiled by Tom Reiter, head coach at Washington and
Jefferson College. Endorsed by Purdue coach Gene Keady, Utah coach
Rick Majerus and former Marquette coach Al McGuire.

$12.95 • paper • 128 pages • diagrams throughout

ISBN: 0-940279-60-6

Coaching Basketball: The Official Centennial Volume of the National Association of Basketball Coaches

Edited by Jerry Krause

New edition! The ultimate reference book for all basketball coaches, this is the compilation of more than 130 articles by the nation's leading coaches at the professional, college and high school levels. No coach who takes his or her job seriously should be without it!

Includes the following chapters:

★ The Birth of the Game (James Naismith)

★ Thoughts on Coaching (Al McGuire)

★ Daily Practice (John Wooden)

★ Organization of Practice and Season (Chuck Daly)

★ Timeouts and Substitutions (Dean Smith)

★ Concern for Players (Mike Krzyzewski)

★ Anatomy of a Rebound (George Raveling)

★ Post Play (John Thompson)

★ Zone Attacks (Jud Heathcote)

★ Pressing Principles (Jerry Tarkanian)

★ Match-up Press Defense (Rick Pitino)

★ A Game Plan (Bob Knight)

$19.95 • paper • 384 pages • diagrams throughout

ISBN: 0-940279-86-X

Five-Star Basketball Drills

Edited by Howard Garfinkel

Includes 131 of the best conditioning and skill drills from Five-Star, the nation's premier basketball camp. A star-studded galaxy of coaches, including Mike Krzyzewski, Rick Pitino and Bob Knight, share the activities that have proven successful year after year at Five-Star.

$14.95 • paper • 256 pages • fully illustrated

ISBN: 0-940279-22-3